Philosophical Adventures with Fairy Tales

The *Big Ideas for Young Thinkers Book Series* brings together the results of recent research about precollege philosophy. There has been sizable growth in philosophy programs for young people. The book series provides readers with a way to learn about all that is taking place in this important area of philosophical and educational practice. It brings together work from around the globe by some of the foremost practitioners of philosophy for children. The books in the series include single-author works as well as essay collections. With a premium placed on accessibility, the book series allows readers to discover the exciting world of precollege philosophy.

Philosophical Adventures with Fairy Tales

New Ways to Explore Familiar Tales with Kids of All Ages

Wendy C. Turgeon

ROWMAN & LITTLEFIELD
Lanham • Boulder • New York • London

Published by Rowman & Littlefield
An imprint of The Rowman & Littlefield Publishing Group, Inc.
4501 Forbes Boulevard, Suite 200, Lanham, Maryland 20706
www.rowman.com

6 Tinworth Street, London SE11 5AL, United Kingdom

Copyright © 2020 by Wendy C. Turgeon

All rights reserved. No part of this book may be reproduced in any form or by any electronic or mechanical means, including information storage and retrieval systems, without written permission from the publisher, except by a reviewer who may quote passages in a review.

British Library Cataloguing in Publication Information Available

Library of Congress Cataloging-in-Publication Data Available

ISBN 9781475853223 (cloth)
ISBN 9781475853230 (pbk.)
ISBN 9781475853247 (electronic)

I dedicate this book to Hazel, Lorelei, and Penelope, my three fairy princesses who will surely make their own ways in the world but with grace, creativity, and an appreciation for the question, "Why?"

Contents

Foreword by Thomas Wartenberg		ix
Acknowledgments		xi
Introduction		1
1	Philosophy Is for Kids!	3
PART I: PHILOSOPHY, DIALOGUE, AND FAIRY TALES		**9**
2	Planning a Philosophical Conversion: A How-To Manual	11
3	Why Fairy Tales?	19
PART II: FAIRY TALES		**25**
4	Introduction to Our Fairy Tales	27
5	*The Frog King* or *Iron Heinrich*	29
6	*Rapunzel*	41
7	*Fitcher's Bird*	51
8	*Little Red Riding Hood*	61
9	*The White Snake*	69
10	*The Little Mermaid*	77
11	*The Seven Ravens*	87
12	*Cinderella*	97

13	*Beauty and the Beast*	107
14	*Hansel and Gretel*	117
15	*Snow White*	133
16	*Master Cat* or *Puss 'n Boots*	141
17	*The Story of the Three Little Bears*	151

Appendix A: For More Information about Philosophy and Children	157
Appendix B: Contemporary Reimaginings of Classic Fairy Tales	161
Appendix C: Themes in Each Fairy Tale	163
Some Notes on Our Sources	167
About the Author	169

Foreword

Many of us have been acquainted with fairy tales since we were very young. *Cinderella*, *Goldilocks and the Three Bears*, and *Snow White* are staples of many childhoods. But rarely, if ever, have we even noticed that many philosophical issues are raised by these tales.

All that will change for those who read Wendy Turgeon's imaginative and creative new book, *Philosophical Adventures with Fairy Tales*. With great skill and ingenuity, Turgeon takes us through thirteen different fairy tales, many of them familiar but some of them not so, showing how these tales raise issues that call for thoughtful discussion. While some of these issues stem from the structure of the tales themselves—Why do things always happen in threes, such as the three bears whose home Goldilocks falls asleep in?—others are explicitly philosophical—as when Turgeon asks us to consider what makes something "just right," as Goldilocks found baby bear's dish, chair, and bed.

There are many different ways that have been suggested as appropriate for introducing children to philosophy. I have advocated using picture books; others have written their own books; still others present philosophical conundrums without any mediation. But fairy tales are a resource that has been more or less ignored. Turgeon demonstrates that fairy tales, in part because of their witty narratives and their very familiarity, provide excellent opportunities for getting children to think philosophically.

Each of the chapters on the fairy tales provides a summary of the story, a general discussion of the philosophical issues raised, specific questions the children might be asked, and a variety of extension activities to further enhance an appreciation of the issues raised. A teacher or parent who is interested in using fairy tales as a way of initiating philosophical discussion will find an excellent guide in Turgeon and the materials she has provided.

In addition to the thirteen fairy tales, this book includes chapters sketching out the history of this genre as well as the basic format that philosophical discussions need to follow. Even those without significant background in philosophy will be able to lead dialogues by following Turgeon's clear and straightforward instructions and guidance.

If you love fairy tales as much as the rest of us, you will find this book both thought-provoking and stimulating. And you'll be inclined to rush out and find a group of children with whom you can share your fairy tale and then embark on a mind-blowing philosophical dialogue.

—Thomas Wartenberg

Acknowledgments

I would like to acknowledge Thomas Wartenberg for his continued support, encouragement, and his ever-helpful suggestions in making this text better. I must also thank St. Joseph's College, New York, for awarding me a summer grant, which helped support my research on fairy tales. The support of the "philosophy with children" international community has enriched my own understanding of both philosophy and childhood, and many people were inspirational in helping me shape my ideas.

I would be remiss if I did not also thank my freshmen students at St. Joseph's College who contributed to our shared inquiry into fairy tales in our freshman seminar on that topic. Last, but not least, I am deeply appreciative of Alice Gerhardstein for her creative and provocative illustrations that themselves invite inquiry.

Introduction

Welcome to the wonderful world of fairy tales! Perhaps you remember them fondly from your youth or you are reading them to your children now. Maybe you are doing a unit on fairy tales in your classroom—which could be anywhere from kindergarten through high school. Fairy tales have a universal appeal, and while the Disney franchise has brought them into our homes and given us iconic images of the characters, this book will invite you to explore the older versions of familiar tales.

The book is divided into two main parts, which do not have to be read sequentially. In Part I you will find an introduction to the ways in which children, even very young children, enjoy philosophical inquiry and how adults can regain their own childlike philosophical self. Chapter 2 will offer some guidelines to introducing philosophy to children and young people—or to adults themselves—in ways which promote deep reflection and genuine dialogue.

Chapter 3 will explain how fairy tales offer wonderful opportunities to have those philosophical discussions and includes a brief history of the fairy tales. You might be intrigued by how fairy tales have evolved over the centuries.

In Part II you will find individual chapters dedicated to specific fairy tales, some familiar but others perhaps new to the readers. Each chapter will offer themes to start your philosophical adventure along with question prompts and often activities. These activities are sometimes geared toward younger children and sometimes teens and adults. Feel free to adapt to suit your own interest and audience. You can read these chapters in any order.

The format of discussion questions and activities was inspired by the work of the Institute for the Advancement of Philosophy for Children, which produced elaborate teachers manuals for their crafted philosophical novels for children. I am deeply indebted to their creative approach to using stories for exploring philosophy.

At the end, you will find three appendices that will offer suggestions for more resources about doing philosophy with children and young people, a short list of contemporary spins on the old fairy tales, and a summary list of the themes in each chapter's fairy tale in case you wish to focus on a particular concept or topic.

We tend to think of philosophy as a college subject accessible only to the few who can comprehend complicated texts. Prepare to be surprised how even simple fairy tales raise the same issues and challenges we find in the great works of philosophy.

Chapter 1

Philosophy Is for Kids!

The purpose of this book is to invite you to rediscover philosophical wonderment with your child or young person (or within yourself). Our vehicle toward this goal will be familiar, and maybe some not-so-familiar, fairy tales. This chapter will offer you some guidelines for building an enjoyable and productive philosophical dialogue and outline strategies to use with children from preschoolers up to adults.

Perhaps you are a parent or relative; you are looking for ways to promote your child's thoughtful disposition and joy of inquiry. You might be a teacher with a full class of children or middle schoolers and you are looking for ways to engage them and help them think carefully and caringly, mastering the techniques of respectful dialogue. Maybe you are running a philosophy club for teens, or are a member of one, and are looking for new ways to explore the big ideas. And finally, perhaps you are an adult who remembers fairy tales fondly and would like to revisit them to see what so captivated you as a child.

This book will offer you ways to have genuine and meaningful conversations with and among children and young people focusing on difficult and genuinely important concepts. It is not a book about the history of philosophy or philosophers. While that could be a great book to read, this book will use fairy tales to provoke genuine philosophical discussions. We will talk a bit more about fairy tales in the chapter 3 but the important point here is that you need not be an expert in philosophical history or ideas to engage in philosophical discussion or to help young people do likewise.

THE CHILD AS A NATURAL PHILOSOPHER

Philosophy is often a subject matter that is relegated to the college level. We may have had a philosophy class in college and found it abstract, complicating, and perhaps too alien for us to grasp. Or perhaps we loved it but could not see any value to it other than the acquiring of a lot of questions with few, if any, answers. Certainly at the precollege level we might assume that philosophy is far too abstract and remote for children to comprehend, and we may worry that teens may find it unsettling or a way to challenge our adult viewpoints.

You may be surprised to learn that children are natural philosophers. Within the past thirty to forty years, there has been a quiet revolution where philosophers have discovered that even very young children, three- and four-year-olds, ask some classic philosophical questions and are genuinely interested in finding answers. The philosopher Gareth Matthews has written some engaging accounts of the kinds of philosophical questions that children entertain, and he introduced traditional philosophical puzzles to children to explore. In his books *Philosophy and the Young Child* and *Dialogues with Children*, Matthews shares many anecdotal examples of serious topics being tackled by children, with surprisingly sophisticated responses.

Another philosopher, Matthew Lipman, was struck by how public education seemed to be failing children and killing the spark of curiosity that they brought to kindergarten. Could philosophy keep that sense of wonder and puzzlement about the world alive? He thought yes and developed an entire curriculum, from preschool through high school, which introduced children and young people to thinking philosophically through discussing carefully crafted stories in which he had embedded traditional philosophical problems and questions.

His goal was to offer young people the chance to learn the skills of inquiry and discussion across a range of different responses. These skills of critical and creative thinking are essential for life in a democracy, he argued. Citizens need to be questioning but open to reason and capable of collegial arguments with a shared goal of finding the best answer or solution to the present problem. I doubt any of us would argue that this is indeed a worthy and necessary goal.

Since these pioneer writers, many others, from around the world, have offered rich academic studies of childhood as philosophically interesting and children as legitimate philosophers. Philosophy with children and philosophy of childhood has become an area of recognized interest among professional philosophers. But teachers and parents have also become increasingly intrigued by the philosophical curiosity of children. As we interact with the children and young people in our lives, we discover how curious and thoughtful they are and we begin to develop new respect for the child.

Despite the common claims that young children cannot think abstractly, we find that they do this all the time. The mastery of even basic language skills reveals generalized thinking. And as Canadian educator Kieran Egan has noted (in *the Educated Mind*), the young child absolutely gets the major themes behind their favorite Disney movie or story. Young children, Egan claims, grasp the world through large binary concepts: good/evil, beauty/ugliness, human/animal, dark/light, princess/witch, and so on.

As soon as children begin to speak, they begin to operate with abstract ideas and are fascinated by the world around them. The quintessential "why" questions of the two- to four-year-olds may be annoying at times but they also reveal a deep thirst to understand, to make meaning of what surrounds them. Aristotle begins his treatise called *The Metaphysics* by saying "All men [humans] by nature desire to know." Clearly, that fascination with the world and meaning is there from the start. So, why is it that we so often get bored and lose our philosophical sense of curiosity?

Why is philosophy so interesting to children and young people and how might it enhance both family engagement and classroom thinking? The rest of this chapter will outline what a philosophical conversation would look like and invite you, the reader, to adapt ideas here to suit your children or young people—or your own thinking.

WHY PHILOSOPHICAL TOPICS INTEREST CHILDREN AND YOUNG PEOPLE

Children and young people are fascinated by the big questions: why do I exist? Where did everything come from? What is the truth? Do numbers really never end? What makes me, *me*? What is the right thing to do and why? These kinds of questions are represented in the traditional areas of philosophy.

In a typical philosophy class one might encounter epistemology, metaphysics, ethics, and aesthetics. What do these terms mean? Epistemology explores how we know about the world and what truth means. Metaphysics tackles questions about the nature and source of reality and the concept of the self, the very meaning of existence. And ethics deals with questions about good and bad, right and wrong, and how we might argue for establishing these normative concepts governing human action. To wonder about beauty is to engage in aesthetics, the study of the concept of the beautiful and the nature of art and creativity. All of these topics are important for children and for adults.

Rules and regulations affect children's lives, and these notions are tackled in political philosophy and ethics. The history of philosophical thinking from the pre-Socratic philosophers in ancient Greece to contemporary philosophers of mind offers many different responses to these tantalizing questions, and we find the same breadth of diverse answers in Asian philosophy from the time of Confucius to now. Philosophy is one of those areas of human reflection that we never outgrow.

Philosophy offers the essential open questioning about the world. While open-ended questions really annoy adults—we want to know what the answers are so we can move on—children appear to be fascinated by the questions themselves and the range of diverse answers excites them precisely because they invite ongoing reflection. These are genuine questions; they are not traps to check on a child's knowledge as measured by a book or the adult authority. We are on equal footing with children while doing philosophy, even if we happen to know a lot more about the type of responses offered by great philosophical minds.

Children can enjoy ambiguity far more comfortably than we give them credit because it signals to them that their questions are valuable, living, and therefore are exciting. Adults sometimes worry that such open-endedness will confuse or upset children who are looking for answers and certainty. And true, there are some questions that really do seek confirmation and reassurance that adults are in control and all is right. But as we shall see, some of these most fundamental and significant human questions in our search for meaning lack that clear and recognizable path to *THE* answer. That is not automatically a hopeless or bad thing.

Not only is it important that adults learn some "epistemic humility," but it can also be liberating for children to find themselves as shared partners in inquiry with the adults in their lives. As much as we want to protect children from the unknown, from the scary, and from doubt, adults must realize that being humble in the face of uncertainty and being willing to submit one's own answers to review is an essential part of being human and being open to better thinking. This highlights the "dialogic" nature of genuine philosophical conversation. We are all in this together.

Being able to revisit ideas that seemed settled is the sign of an open mind and a truly human talent for revision and improvement; this can lead to mental and personal growth. While we may hold fast to the worldview we have inherited from our own family and upbringing, we must admit that we do not simply blindly adopt everything our parents and grandparents taught us. We adults had to choose to embrace the way we see the world and even if we are certain that this is the exact worldview we want our children to share, we must allow them to make that choice for themselves. But as adults we too continue to grow and change.

What we can do to help children is allow them to question, explore, but to do so with critical and caring thinking. This is where we can join them in philosophical reflection and find, perhaps to our surprise, that meaning-making never ends. We ourselves can learn from engaging in inquiry with our children, whether they are our own or an entire class. So what does this kind of inquiry look like and how can we avoid both confusing children and perhaps "indoctrinating" them with ideas for which they might not be ready?

We recognize that both of these concerns are real. We do not want to confuse children or young people to the point where they feel helpless or worried about themselves and the world. Likewise, in a philosophical dialogue we want to follow the example of Socrates and try to avoid pushing ideas on them, especially if they are not ready for them. This might be of particular concern to parents who hear of schools introducing their children to philosophy. Will they be taught the *right* philosophy, they may wonder. The methods proposed here consciously seek to avoid both of these problematic outcomes.

If the children are driving the philosophical dialogue through their questions and chosen topics, we can avoid having adults push an "agenda" on them. If the children are interested in an idea, it means that they are already thinking about it. In the discussion plans in the fairy tale chapters, themes are suggested but mostly as a guide for the facilitator to listen for the theme to emerge from the children and young people discussing the tale. While some confusion can be good, the facilitator must be alert to any topic that veers too close to the personal or seems to genuinely upset the discussants.

The following chapter will offer guidelines for having a meaningful and productive philosophical dialogue with very young children, middle-school children, and teens. Of course, many of these topics are equally interested to an adult group so consider having a "Fairy tale evening" with friends to explore the rich themes found in these stories.

Part I

PHILOSOPHY, DIALOGUE, AND FAIRY TALES

Chapter 2

Planning a Philosophical Conversion: A How-To Manual

WHAT DOES PHILOSOPHY AT THE PRECOLLEGE LEVEL LOOK LIKE?

This chapter will offer some concrete advice on how to organize and facilitate a philosophical dialogue with your children. Let's begin by noting that having a philosophical conversation with children is not about teaching them the history of philosophy nor is it necessarily reading dense philosophical prose. In fact it is not strictly teaching them at all, that is, if you think of teaching as conveying important information for students to learn and master. But it is also not simply chatting about topics with no direction and goal or standards by which to explore the problem at hand. A philosophical conversation requires a willingness to follow the question with attention to the logic of response.

While a philosophical conversation could start with an offhand remark or question while traveling in a car or on a bus, it can also be provoked by events or situations that puzzle or surprise us. Using stories to provoke philosophical puzzlement is a proven technique to access rich and rewarding philosophical dialogue. Many children and young adult fiction stories invite just these kinds of explorations—if we know how to start them.

This book will provide a range of philosophical ideas that are buried in traditional fairy tales. Fairy tales offer particularly enticing opportunities to explore familiar stories and themes but in new and exciting ways. The next chapter will introduce you to fairy tales and why they are rich sources for philosophy.

Here are some general guidelines to follow based on loose age groupings. Of course, adapt these based on situation and your children or young people. Your philosophical conversation can take place between you and your child, with a group of children, even with mixed ages, or in a classroom or philosophy club.

PRESCHOOL UP THROUGH ELEMENTARY GRADE YEARS

1. Find a quiet time when you can be relatively undisturbed, and you can focus on the child or children. Schedule your discussions—not as chores but to be sure that they do not get missed or lost in the business of our contemporary lives.
2. Invite your child or a group to have fun with philosophy! Tell them philosophy is about asking questions, exploring different answers, and looking for puzzles.
3. Choose one of our fairy tales as discussed in this text. Read it out loud to them or have them read it; if you are working with a group of children have them read it in turns while sitting in a circle.
4. Stop at every page or when you sense they found something funny, confusing, puzzling, or they simply want to ask a question.
5. Always listen to what your child or young person has to say. Do not rush to correct them, tell them what they mean, or what they should think. Ask them to explain or define their words.
6. Remember that this activity is not about reading comprehension but rather following ideas where they take us. Ideas can be like beautiful birds that start off in a bush but fly up in the sky and we follow them, forgetting about the bush. So don't worry about staying within the story line. This willingness to follow ideas outside of the story differentiates a philosophy discussion from a reading lesson. Reading lessons are fine and helpful but make sure that you convey to the children that they are on a philosophical adventure and it is perfectly OK to not worry as much about the story itself. It is about what the story makes us think of.
7. It can be helpful to write down children's comments or questions at some point so that you end up with a list of potential discussion topics. You can invite them to suggest anything that puzzled them, confused them, was interesting, or something it made them think of—even it if has nothing to do with the story.
8. Try to start with their questions first. This allows them to shape the discussion based on what interests them, rather than what interested you. Some of the questions may be content-based and it will take practice to be alert to the questions with the most potential for philosophy. That is part of the value of having the outlined discussion plans and themes that appear in the latter part of this book. They can help you tune your own ears for potentially rich topics to explore.
9. Don't be afraid to ask for alternative viewpoints. Make it clear that we are interested in all answers and ideas; we are not looking for just one response. If everyone agrees, pose an alternative viewpoint or response to see if that might solicit some attention. With very young children, it is

common that the first answer is readily adopted by all. So you may need to work on getting them to explore alternatives.
10. With our fairy tales you may choose to read the whole story first and then solicit questions and comments for their "discussion agenda" or you may wish to stop at a particular part of the story. This is up to you and your co-inquirers.
11. Your role is to facilitate the discussion or, if just you and your child, be a true-co-inquirer. Focus on asking reasons for their answers, solicit counterexamples or potential other responses that someone could say. Help them think about their own answers and why they work, or what problems they might have. Be careful not to answer for them or rush to give them your viewpoint. Let them play with the ideas or questions that emerged. When they seem to want to move on, let them do so. Perhaps the question has run its course or they want to get back to the story or look at another point of interest.
12. Enjoy your child or children and watch how they blossom as their ideas are counted as important and significant.
13. Have fun!

Depending on the age of the children, this conversation may last fifteen minutes or an hour. There is no perfect length of time. But do not hesitate to revisit the questions next time you decide to have a philosophical conversation. A conversation about one fairy tale could last a day or a week, or maybe even longer.

MIDDLE SCHOOL TO HIGH SCHOOL AGE

While the general pattern of the discussion will remain the same, older children and young adults may wish to springboard more quickly outside the story to connect ideas to their own lives. Since this is not a reading comprehension lesson, using fairy tales, supposedly the stuff of early childhood interest, can offer them a "stress free" entrance into philosophical reflection. Older children may scoff at fairy tales, but you might also discover that they find it delightful to explore philosophical ideas hidden in such "baby books." In many tales the themes are far from limited to the interest of children and older children and teens may enjoy exploring these adult topics buried in stories they thought were limited to younger ones.

You can avoid the pressure that young people feel when asked to tackle novels that may present reading challenges for them. Fairy tales are perfect since you can share with older children the history of fairy tales (see chapter 3 in this book) and explain how these stories were written first for adults and entire families to enjoy—not just for little kids. But the familiarity with many fairy tales makes them enjoyable to revisit and explore for new ideas. Since the classic versions recommended here may not be their familiar sources, reading these will surprise them as they compare these tales with the movie and television versions.

Use the same format of reading together and writing down the ideas that the stories suggest to the young people. The discussion plans in this book offer some topics that are clearly better suited to older children than very young ones but many of the ideas suggested work well for all ages, including for adults to think about. The discussion plans indicate where a theme might be more appropriate or accessible to teens and adults. With older children, you may find them willing to entertain a range of possible responses and ideas, but you do not want to leave them with the conclusion that anything goes. Giving good reasons for their views is critical to the nature of a dialogue as philosophical.

Again, the length of the conversation depends upon the attention span and dedication of your young person(s). Do not feel as if you must spend a certain amount of time discussing a topic. If the children and young adults own the discussion, it is more likely to continue with enthusiasm than if the adults set the agenda. Bear that in mind. This also avoids the experience as seeming to be a teaching of ideas by an adult.

KEY ASPECTS TO HELP YOU PLAN YOUR DISCUSSION

Some points are shared regardless of the age of our child or of the young people in our philosophy group. A good philosophical discussion has a movement forward. The conclusion could be that what seemed obvious is actually anything but. This is the same lesson often learned in Plato's Socratic dialogues: at the end the friends have discovered what they do *not* know, and in doing this, have become better informed about the options and why some clearly do not work to answer the question or define the term being considered. Knowing that I do not know is itself an achievement of philosophical reflection. And it encourages the participant to keep thinking!

But part of the dialogic process involves careful attention to the form of the discussion. When are we giving examples versus definitions? Often our first attempt to define a troublesome idea is to offer examples: a friend is like my bestie, John. But examples are concrete and not general as a definition must be. What do all friends have in common that make them friends? Here we are looking for key criteria to help us understand the concept of "friend."

Are we explaining something that is clearly happening or are we arguing that something might or will happen? Explanations are causal in nature and start with an existing fact to work backward to offer clues as to why it is such as it is. Predictions look to the future and may be more or less certain based on the evidence we supply.

Are our statements descriptions or prescriptions? Descriptions can be detailed and important to understanding an event or idea but the fact that something is this way does not automatically mean it should be that way. "Everybody lies" may be a true description of human beings (although you might wish to disagree), but assuming it is true does not justify lying. Explaining or describing the history of prejudice in a country does not suffice to justify it as inevitable or as acceptable because "that is what we think or do."

Do our premises lead incontrovertibly to the conclusion (deductive reasoning) or do they offer strong support for it (inductive reasoning?) Most of the arguments we encounter are inductive in nature. We offer evidence that is hopefully so compelling that we are confident that our position is a strong one. Science operates on the basis of inductive reasoning. The more all the evidence points to a theory being applicable, the more confident we are in its strength or truth value.

Deductive reasoning is pure logic: if the premises are true, then a sound deductive argument leads incontrovertibly to its conclusion. These kinds of arguments may be less applicable in real life, but they work like a charm if we find one. For a simple but effective example, consider these claims: if it is raining outside, I will wear my boots to work. It is raining outside. Assuming both are true, can you figure out what I have on my feet? Right—boots!

In a lively philosophical dialogue, we want to be sure to explore all options. When we all agree, can we think of arguments for the other side? Here the facilitator or the participants can entertain "what if" scenarios. What might be another position and how could someone support that one? How would we meet challenges to our definition or position? We don't want to agree too quickly as the group might miss another idea or response. These are all hallmarks of being good critical thinkers.

This very conscious attention to the form of argumentation is essential for building a philosophical community. The shared focus is on the "arguments" before the group, not the people. Remember, in the context, an 'argument" is not a fight but a way to present evidence to support a claim. However, we must listen respectfully to any position offered and devote our attention to the presented support, not scoffing at reasons because of their source.

So, while a topic might be "what is beauty?" we are dealing with both the question itself and the possible responses as well as the process of engaging in the inquiry. Not all opinions are equally valuable when scrutinized by our philosophers. We must be open to all responses, but we are not obliged to accept them all or treat them as equally well supported by evidence and reasons.

So, to summarize, a philosophical conversation is prompted by reading a story (for our purposes here, a fairy tale) and inviting the children to come up with an agenda of questions or topics that the story presented to them as interesting, puzzling, or simply fun to pursue. Once they have created the agenda, the facilitator, you, can help them shape their conversation by reminding them of the rules of logic, posing questions to move their thinking forward or to introduce alternative ideas.

At the end, it is well worth having the group do a debriefing:

- What did we discover?
- What questions remain for us to continue to ponder?
- Did we listen to one another with respect?
- Did we offer reasons for what we said?
- Did we explore facts or values?
- Did everyone get a chance to offer his or her view?

This final meta-reflection helps our young philosophers appreciate the level of thinking in which they have engaged and can help them fine-tune their own sensitivity to the types of questions and ideas we explore. Even if no final answers were found or agreed upon, they can appreciate the quality of their thinking and the discussion.

THE VALUE OF PHILOSOPHY IN THE SCHOOLS

This book is designed for multiple uses. As suggested, we could be having a dialogue with our own child while sitting at the dinner table or driving to baseball practice. Teachers might find this a valuable resource for an enhanced version of story time, but now it is "philosophy time." What we can claim, with some studies to support it, is that encouraging children to ask difficult questions and self-reflectively grow their reasoning and inquiry abilities and skills pays off in better academic performance but also importantly in a more engaged young person. Education cannot be simply about information loading—even if knowing "stuff" provides valuable support when building arguments and trying to understand the world around us.

While "rote learning" has been denigrated in recent educational circles, there remains genuine value in having a cache of information that one can call upon in sorting out experiences. But if all we ask of children is that they memorize and be able to parrot that information back, we have failed to educate them. Children need to learn what information matters and how to evaluate the enormous amount of data thrown their way from all angles now (the Internet being a major source that previous generations did not have).

But they also need what to do with it and in the process of evaluating what they are taught, we want them to own their own education, to tackle difficult concepts and work toward meaning-making. When that happens, the knowledge acquired becomes useful for more than exams or playing *Jeopardy* on TV. Even the information and values shared by family and teachers deserve careful scrutiny—not to unduly challenge the adults in children's lives but to offer them the invaluable chance to appreciate the truth value of what we hold to be true and good.

If parents and teachers have sound information backed by good arguments, we want our children to be able to appreciate that and embrace them. Otherwise, we are left with the authoritarian insistence on conformity without understanding and this can backfire with young people rejecting good ideas simply because they are pushing back against the adult authoritarians in their lives. We want our views to be authoritative (through good reasoning and evidence) not simply authoritarian (through brute power.)

Philosophy in the home and in the classroom builds this degree of trust between co-inquirers and equips our children with skills of reasoning and listening, an openness to self-correction, and seeing learning and knowledge as a collaborative endeavor of utmost importance for all of us. The essence of a critical thinker is not only to be able to think logically but to be able to communicate ideas and listen to alternative positions since everything merits from reflection and revisiting, even our most cherished beliefs.

While consistency is a value, it becomes a vice when it merges into a stubborn refusal to be open to better ideas, more grounded reasoning, and the potential that one might be mistaken. Being fallible is not a failing but rather a sign of deep epistemic humility and courage. Philosophy can remind us that the wisest among us, much like Socrates, is so because she knows she does not know. But at the same time, she reaches out to know more and know better.

HOW PARENTS CAN ENJOY PHILOSOPHY WITH THEIR CHILDREN

Parents reading this book can discover the joys of genuine conversations with their children. Philosophy can bring adult and child together to explore important concepts that both care deeply about and they can share these intellectual adventures. We often bemoan how busy life is today and how children and young adults are always on the run to sports, lessons, work, or play dates.

Parents struggle to balance their work lives with home and children. Life is challenging, for certain. So an opportunity to stop and talk with one another can be an invaluable gift for both parent and child. What a great opportunity to put down our cell phones, pull out those ear buds, walk away from the TV, Xbox, or computer, and simply converse with one another.

Of course, these conversations can also happen in the car or on the bus as you accompany your child to their activities. Philosophical dialogues can happen at the dinner table or before bedtime. Once you have had a chance to practice asking philosophical questions and exploring possible answers, philosophy turns out to be quite portable! And don't forget to include your child's friends in on the fun. Many children have no adults to talk to as we seem to live in a more age-segregated society. An adult who truly listens to children and young people can be a powerful force for good in their lives as can they in the adults' lives.

SUMMARY

Regardless of your age, philosophy is for everyone and melding philosophical inquiry with fairy tales offers all of us a wonderful opportunity to explore meaning-making in our lives through these fictional and magical scenarios. The following chapter will explore why fairy tales for philosophical dialogue. Many fairy tales introduce social justice issues, questions about gender roles, and key ethical ideas such as honesty, promises, good, and evil.

While this book offers thirteen tales, you can easily introduce other fairy tales and adapt the thematic questions and activities to new stories. Above all, philosophy is serious but also playful and fun. Get ready for an adventure in thinking.

Chapter 3

Why Fairy Tales?

Fairy tales are familiar to most of us. Growing up we loved hearing the stories of princesses and princes as well as talking animals, magical wishes, and often scary stories with witches and ogres. We may fondly remember our favorite Disney movie from our childhood or enjoy watching with children the new Disney movies that come out on a regular basis. "Fairy tales" is a recognized genre of children's literature.

We may think of fairy tales as too simple, too childish, and therefore not worth much serious attention, much less philosophical dialogue. But "Once upon a time" can captivate old and young. This makes fairy tales particularly attractive for engaging children, young people, and even adults in reflective thinking. These stories reveal themselves to be not simple mundane kiddie fare. We discover a world of big ideas buried in the simple and entertaining story lines. More about those big ideas in a minute.

A BRIEF HISTORY OF FAIRY TALES AND THE MYSTERIES SURROUNDING THEM

Let's take a short detour to explore the origins of these tales. The history of European fairy tales is a long and conflicted one. Fairy tales as a genre date back to the sixteenth century with writers/collectors such as Giambattista Basile and Straparola in Italy. In the sixteenth century, these tales were written for an adult audience and tended to be bawdy, irreverent, and replete with sexual innuendo. The language can be crude and certainly not what we associate with children's stories. In many versions they poke fun at people in power and celebrate the peasant who wins over the prince. Indeed, under the cloak of a story, a fiction, one can be highly critical of people and situations where it might be dangerous to do so as a political statement. But this all happened long ago and far away—the safeguard of the storyteller.

In seventeenth- and eighteenth-century France, aristocratic writers such as Madame d'Aulnoy, Madame de Sevigne, and Charles Perrault transformed these tales into amusements for salons, gatherings of wealthy aristocrats seeking to be entertained. Perrault's tales usually had a very contemporary and pointed moral at the end of the story. Some of our most beloved stories, such as *Beauty and the Beast* and *Little Red Riding Hood*, received linguistically rich treatments from these writers. The moral of the story was clearly stated but often with an air of ironic amusement. The stories have been cleaned up considerably from the earlier peasant versions but, nevertheless, often include an erotic and violent edge to them. Yet they were often claimed as stories told to the writers as children by their nannies or "mother goose."

Perhaps we owe our most familiar versions of fairy tales to the dedication of Jacob and Wilhelm Grimm. In the nineteenth century, these two brothers devoted their full time to collecting what they considered genuine tales of the German folk. Throughout the nineteenth century they edited and published seven editions of their Grimm's *Kinder und Haus Märchen*. Their work stands as one of the most important avenues for the introduction of fairy tales into our lives and that of our children.

One of their goals was to create a German identity through storytelling. As Napoleon was besieging the Germanic states, the Grimm brothers were eager to forge a sense of a united German past and stories seemed like a way to achieve this, although it is worth noting that many of their stories are borrowed from non-German sources. They insisted these tales came from uneducated folk, but the reality is probably quite different. One of their main sources was an educated governess in a middle-class family. This helps to explain why tales found in French and Italian sources reappear as German fairy tales.

As they expanded and changed the collection in the revised editions, they also edited and changed the tales, making them more "child-friendly" and useful as moral educational devices. They envisioned their book as a critical text not only for building national pride but also instilling key virtues in young children. But the changes they made could lead to some odd results.

One example from Rapunzel is worth noting. In the first edition Rapunzel comments innocently to her witch keeper that her clothes are getting tighter. The witch immediately understands that some man has been visiting her. In later editions Rapunzel asks her why the old woman is so much heavier than the prince to pull up. The first version reveals how innocent and unknowing Rapunzel is, while the revised version seems to depict her as a ninny, but it avoids any reference to being pregnant! The Grimm's versions of the fairy tales and folktales quickly became household staples and were used as key literary sources for moral education of young children.

The audience and nature of fairy tales has changed over the centuries and in fact what constitutes a fairy tale is contested hotly today. Ruth Bottigheimer of Stony Brook University argues that they were invented as literary entertainment in Venice in the sixteenth century for the merchant caste. This would pull them out of the misty folk past and put them as urban creations.

The more commonly accepted theory is that they originated in oral traditions around Europe and the Middle East and traveled along trade routes, being "naturalized" and integrated into the receiving culture in each location. This might explain why so many variations of the tales exist and appear in other traditions as noted earlier.

WHAT MAKES A FAIRY TALE A FAIRY TALE?

Trying to define a fairy tale is itself a challenging enterprise. In fact, very seldom are fairies involved. We do find magic, imaginary lands ("long ago and far away"), talking animals, and usually a happy ending. While myths can end in tragedy, fairy tales often end with living happily ever after. But not always—the Grimm's collection includes a number of tragic stories with the heroes or heroines dying at the end. In the 1920s, the Russian scholar Vladimir Propp developed an elaborate morphology of folk/fairy tales which categorized them into complex groupings based on the characters and events.

Many fairy tales tell the story of a hero or heroine who must meet adversities and overcome them to win in the end. In stories these heroes are often ordinary people who win great fortune and fame through being clever and kind with a dose of magic to help them succeed. That success is usually measured in wealth, love, and general happiness.

This message resonates with all of us, regardless of our age, social caste, or culture. Magical thinking is alive and well in twenty-first-century industrialized countries. However, we also find a strong theme for justice where evil stepsisters, mothers, and jealous siblings are punished in the end for their evil ways. The happy ending in a fairy tale can be quite violent but it is toward those who truly seem to deserve such punishment.

THE MYSTERIOUS MEANINGS BEHIND FAIRY TALES

But not only is the historical background of fairy tales a bit mysterious, recently serious scholars have sought to decode their meaning through a wide range of readings and interpretations as well. A tale might receive quite different interpretations at the hands of these individuals. Scholars from diverse disciplines, such as psychology, history, literature, and social theory, have all investigated the tantalizing power of the fairy tale. Why do they persist both in the culture and through history but also in our own memories? It can be both fun and instructive to explore these wildly different takes on what fairy tales are really about.

The psychiatrist Bruno Bettelheim in his *The Uses of Enchantment* (1976) presented fairy tales as vehicles for children to work through difficult psychological transition phases in their lives and to displace anger at parents onto the figures of evil stepmothers and witches or ogres. He adopts a Freudian lens to analyze tales such as *Hansel and Gretel* and *Bluebeard* to highlight how these stories are really vehicles for children to work through their subconscious fear of abandonment or apprehension about sex.

In his readings, the power of the fairy tale for young children lay in its ability to help them work through periods of sexual anxiety and deal with feelings, positive and negative, about their parents. His book has been soundly criticized as sexist in many of his claims; yet it did open up the genre for serious attention. And literature does offer us ways to work through feelings of anger and jealousy in safe ways.

From a literary perspective, Angela Carter,[1] a well-known novelist, rewrote many of the familiar fairy tales with a feminist and very adult twist. Feminists have devoted much attention to deconstructing the meaning of fairy tales and the ways in which girls and women have been depicted therein. Are fairy tale girls and women passively waiting for a prince to save them? To what extent are they property to be exchanged between father and husband, even if the husband is a beast? Carter's tales spin the storyline to depict the women as strong and ultimately triumphing over their male oppressors, often through bonding with other women.

Movies based on fairy tales offer a provocative source of material for critique, especially regarding the messages sent to young girls and boys about gender and power. But we find movies also taking the fairy tale trope and turning it on its head or raising questions about the traditional course of fairy tale events. Disney movies have shifted from the princess needing rescuing (*Sleeping Beauty*) to the princess being a plucky and capable heroine (*Frozen*). And yet feminine beauty is tightly defined in these stories and the princess tends to be slim, beautiful, and often blond.

Recently, scholars who dedicated their focus on fairy tales such as Jack Zipes, Marina Warner, and Maria Tartar have analyzed fairy tales through the lens of social theory. Their reflections can shake us up and help the readers expand their own ways of reading the tales, thereby preparing them to be open to problematizing the familiar. That is, they nudge us to see important questions and problems raised by living in society and to tackle these themes as needing careful examination.

These writers challenge us to read each fairy tale as a script for both gender and social roles. In noting these patterns, they invite us to question our own present-day social roles. They point out that in many cases trickery and lying win the day and the clever thief is to be much admired. Likewise, the passive princess who must hope to be rescued teaches girls that their role in society is to serve men as commanded and to be patient, obedient, "good girls."

But every now and then we find the plucky heroine who challenges these models and escapes death by being smarter than the man she married. Those are tales worth noting and several of them are included in the tales that follow.

FAIRY TALES AS PHILOSOPHICAL PROMPTS

Stories have always served not simply as entertainment but also as invitations to explore serious concepts about human life, but fairy tales are rich and too often ignored sources for these questions. Cloaked in story form, we can encounter tough realities such as starvation, abandonment, and even cannibalism. But we also find tales of grace, pluck, compassion, and human goodness. When we begin to notice these big ideas, fairy tales present themselves to us in new and exciting ways—ways which invite philosophical explorations. In the chapters that follow, you will find a wide array of thematic invitations to explore the rich ideas embedded within the familiar plots.

Look for such philosophical themes as nature and the world around us; animals as friends or foes; social justice issues: family, society, and the stranger; gender roles as raising questions; and the classical philosophical questions about truth, beauty, and goodness. It is these big ideas that captivate children and young people as they try to make sense of their experience and their place in the world.

The fictional nature of fairy tales is enhanced by the magical distancing from present times. We can safely regard the characters and events in fairy tales and yet weave connections and applications to our own lived experience. Who has not needed courage to face the unknown dark forests before one? Or wished or dreamed to live quite differently from how one lives? Or experienced cruelty and kindness from others?

Through the fictional lens of the fairy tale, we can not only suspend our belief but also directly confront the challenges with which the characters must grapple and tackle these same experiences in our contemporary lives. Children, teens, and adults can join forces to work together to become better critical thinkers and more caring and aware members of their families and social groups—as well as simply better human beings.

That is the great promise of philosophy and while there are no guarantees that such a transformation will happen, thoughtful and caring human beings always have an edge over the uncaring and thoughtless ones. Fairy tales will offer the readers an adventure in philosophical wonderment along with imaginative and engaging stories.

NOTE

1. https://usa.angelacarter.co.uk.

Part II

FAIRY TALES

Chapter 4

Introduction to Our Fairy Tales

You will find countless sources for the following twelve fairy tales. The classic versions can be found in some of the texts mentioned later, but simplified tales or tales rewritten with young children in mind abound in libraries and bookstores. You might consider avoiding versions with pictures so your audience can imagine themselves in the stories.

However, so many published fairy tales include illustrations that it could be a challenge finding books without them. That said, sometimes pictures themselves can generate a great dialogue of discovery and fairy tale editions have been richly illustrated over the past hundred years, so try using the images themselves as philosophical discussion prompts.

For many readers their first encounter with some of these tales may have been through a Disney movie or cartoon. I urge you to find the original or classic versions of the same story so as to go beyond the movie or television retelling. You will be surprised at how the recent versions have rewritten fairy tales, often in ways that you might want to question.

While our image of Ariel, the little mermaid, Beauty in *Beauty and the Best*, and Snow White have been indelibly set by the iconic Disney movies, the story lines have been made more violent in some cases and sanitized in others. Reading a version captured by the Grimm brothers or the original Hans Christian Andersen may offer your audience some surprises and open up opportunities to question why newer retellings have included the changes they did.

Each following chapter offers a quick plot summary of the story but do not skip reading the language of the Grimm brothers, Charles Perrault, Hans Christian Andersen, and others, even if in translations. A reading guide, age range suggestion, and a number of themes to explore in discussion follow for each tale presented.

Each suggested theme offers a reflective introduction to help you get thinking about the concepts. The purpose of this is to help you develop your "philosophical ear" for problematical concepts and themes. You will find yourself discovering other topics to explore as you practice doing philosophy. The introduction to the theme is followed by discussion questions that can be used to spark philosophical conversation. In some cases, an activity or project is also offered to enrich your exploration of the tale.

Not every theme or discussion plan may be overtly philosophical. To offer variety in encouraging your children and young people to reflect upon big ideas, you will find some themes that invite them to learn more about other topics, for example, animals or history. This allows you all to explore related topics and expand your inquiry beyond strictly philosophical themes. These other themes can lead to philosophical inquiry, perhaps at the instigation of the children themselves. However, most of the ideas presented do encourage participants to address issues deemed to be philosophical.

However, do not feel compelled to choose the themes suggested or be limited by them. The best conversations come from the questions and ideas of your children and young people. In any case, do not see these suggested themes, questions, and activities as something you must work through, like a school workbook. Pick and choose. Many fairy tales introduce the same themes so in the tales included here you will find themes revisited in other tales. This is a powerful way to remind ourselves and our children that great ideas merit another look.

A quick reminder: these tales are not just for kids. Children of all ages, including adults, can find universal themes and big issues. Encourage teens and young adults to take them seriously and truly explore the philosophical questions that will emerge with an imaginative reading. You will find helpful tips on developing philosophical conversation in the earlier chapter on philosophical dialogue.

Finally, each chapter has an image that symbolizes ideas and events from that fairy tale. Consider asking your child or young people to "decode" the image and perhaps create one of their own.

Chapter 5

The Frog King or Iron Heinrich

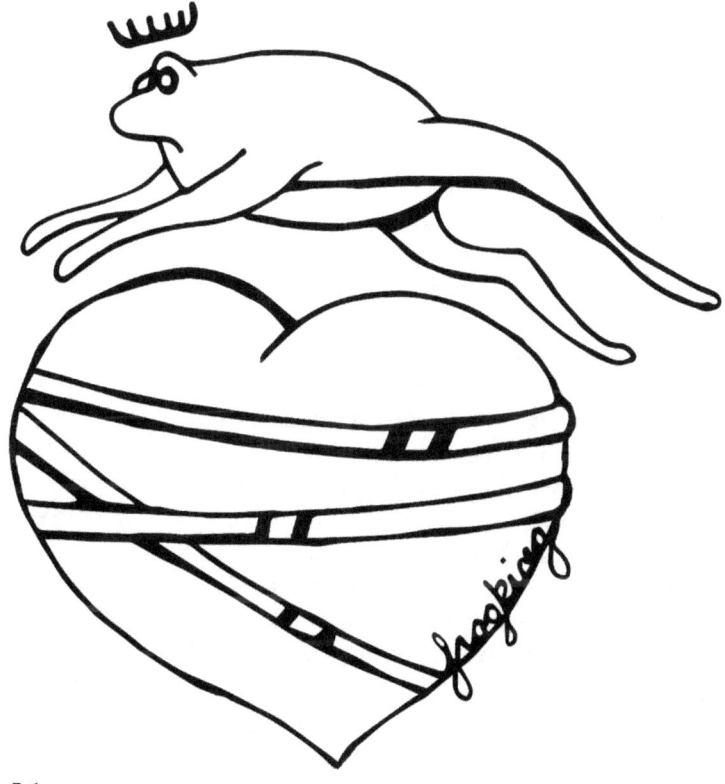

Figure 5.1
Credit Line: Alice V. Gerhardstein

This fairy tale opens the collection of the Brothers Grimm edited by Jack Zipes. You can find it in various versions in other collections. This story has a happy ending but with a curious and rather disturbing twist. You will find a number of places to pause and question the characters' motives and actions.

PLOT

The king's youngest and beautiful daughter goes off to a forest to play and ends up sitting by an old tree near a spring. She tosses her golden ball up in the air and catches it but when she misses, it tumbles into the water and she is dismayed and sobs at losing her favorite toy. A voice asks her what the problem is and she discovers a talking frog sitting by the spring. Instead of being surprised, she takes this in stride and explains that she has lost her favorite toy. He asks her what she would give for its return, and she immediately offers him a number of precious possessions: dresses, jewelry, even her crown.

He replies that none of these will do but that he wants to become her companion and eat from her plate, drink from her cup, and sleep in her bed with her. The princess thinks to herself that this is ridiculous but promises him yes so that he will get her ball and he complies.

The next day while she and her father, the king, are sitting at dinner, they hear a knock on the door and the princess gets up to see who is there. Dismayed to see the disgusting frog she slams the door. When her father asks his daughter what upset her, she explains the events. He insists that a promise is a promise so she must let the frog in. Imagine her feelings when the frog demands to sit on the table and eat from her plate and drink from her cup! She balks at taking him upstairs but her father reminds her that "when someone has helped you, you owe them."

In her room, she puts the nasty frog in the corner, but he asks to be put up on the bed, threatening to tell her father if she does not comply. Yuck, she thinks. At this point, she has had enough. so she throws him violently against the wall. Splat! Here magic happens and the frog is transformed into a handsome young prince. A witch had turned him into a frog and only a princess could save him. Now her feelings change completely!

The next day they marry and ride off in his fabulous carriage. The story ends with his faithful servant sitting in the back of the carriage expressing his happiness at his master's release. Heinrich had bound up his chest with metal bands to prevent his heart from breaking when his master had been turned into a frog by a nasty witch and now one by one the bands burst. This ending seems like a strange add-on to the story but let's think about this.

TARGETED AGE LEVEL: ELEMENTARY THROUGH HIGH SCHOOL

Given that fairy tales were originally written or recited to families and gatherings of mixed ages, it is worth reminding ourselves that we can enjoy fairy tales at any age. If your audience sees them as "baby stories," invite them to take another look and see if they can find ideas that connect to their own experiences.

READING PLAN

There are many editions of the Brothers Grimm's fairy tales; two are listed at the end of this chapter. Read the story out loud or together with the children or young people. As you read the story, pause to solicit some responses, comments, questions from the participants. Watch for reactions from them: giggling, facial expressions that seem puzzled, surprised, or simply reacting to the story. Ask for what interested them, what bothered them, what confused them.

Be alert to words that might be a good prompt for philosophical reflection. What follows are some themes/questions that might come up and suggestions on how to "unpack" their meaning. Do not be afraid to pursue other ideas that your young people offer. And do not feel as if you must work through all of these themes. These are simply suggestions and may be helpful in tuning your own "philosophical ear" for the big ideas in the tale.

THEMES TO EXPLORE

Beauty

How often do we read about beauty in fairy tales? The princess heroine is always a beauty and her "prince charming" is likewise young and handsome. We are attracted to beautiful people and things, even if we know that "beauty is only skin deep." Somehow it still matters as deeply significant. Fairy tales often couple beauty with virtue, although not always. Evil stepmothers are often described as beautiful but cruel. We shall meet some of them in other tales. In our current story, we are told that the young princess is extraordinarily beautiful, but do her actions support a beauty of person? Before offering that contrast, invite the children to reflect on what beauty means.

Discussion Questions

1. Give an example of a person that you would say is beauty. What leads us to say that someone is beautiful? Try listing what qualities that you think beauty needs to be "beautiful."
2. Can anything be beautiful? Beautiful mud? Beautiful hurricane? Beautiful frogs?
3. Is it important to be beautiful? Why or why not?
4. Could someone be beautiful but mean?
5. Could someone be very ugly but a nice person?
6. How do we describe beauty differently for things we see, things we hear, things we smell, touch, and feel?
7. Are being good and being beautiful the same? Why or why not?
8. There is a saying that beauty is only skin deep. What do you think this means? Do you agree? Why or why not?
9. Can I be wrong about claiming that something is beautiful? Why or why not?

Activity

1. Draw a picture of a beautiful princess or prince or write a descriptive paragraph that offers us a word picture. Have the group share their pictures/descriptions and compare to see what common elements are there.
2. Beauty is often framed as a quality of vision; ask the children to offer examples of other appearances of beauty: in music, in smell, in tactile or sense of touch. Have them bring in. Have them display these and, as a community, discuss why they chose that object.

Frogs

Frogs are amphibians and are found all over the world. Many species are born as tadpoles and morph into their recognizable frog shape. Their presence, or absence, serves as an important ecological signal to scientists on the health of their local environment. In this story, we have a talking frog that makes a deal with the princess. In the end, we learn that he was not really a frog at all but a human man under a witch's spell. While the idea of frogs may not be particularly philosophical, there are ways to think about these creatures that open up avenues for reflection.

Discussion Questions

1. Do frogs make good pets? Why or why not?
2. Some people—like the princess—find frogs to be disgusting. What characteristics do they offer to justify their claims?

3. What makes a frog beautiful? Or can a frog be beautiful?
4. What makes a frog to be a good frog? Or a bad one?
5. In the story the frog speaks a human language to communication with the princess; can a frog communicate with you without speaking your language? Why yes or why not?
6. Can we truly understand how the world appears to a frog or another animal unlike us humans? How so or why not?
7. What reasons might we have to caring about frogs?

Activities

1. Fill the following chart and then discuss the results; what do we learn about frogs and humans? As a community, add some other ways to compare frogs and humans to this chart.

Traits	Frogs	Humans
Size		
Smell		
Skin		
Sounds		
communication		
development		
Role in their community		
Length of life		

2. Talking animals are very common in children's stories. Have each child bring in a favorite book that features animals as main characters. Have each participant share the story and then address the following two questions:

   a. Are the animals presented as themselves or more like humans?
   b. Why do you think the author uses animals in this story the way they do?

Making Promises

A key component of this fairy tale is the making and keeping of promises, even when we do not wish to do so. Why is promise-making seen as a key component to being a good person? We often see promise-keeping as a sacred trust that breaking would be unethical. But must we keep all promises?

Are some promises wrong even to attempt to make? In this story, the king insists that his daughter keep her promise but was that fair to her? Was the promise the princess made to the frog a good promise to make? Or is his insistence a strong vote for the importance of being careful what we promise?

Discussion Questions

1. What is a promise?
2. Why are promises generally important to keep?
3. When we make a promise, should we be thinking about the consequences of keeping or breaking the promise?
4. When we make a promise, should we be thinking about our intentions and not be concerned about consequences?
5. Are all promises verbal? Could you make a promise without saying anything?
6. If I think that I will not keep the promise, but I make it anyway, have I lied or not made a promise to begin with?
7. Does the meaning of the promise depend at all on the person to whom I am making a promise? Explain the difference if there is one, for example, promising something to your mother, best friend, teacher, coach, a judge in a court room, a clerk in the store, and so on.
8. Does the promise depend on what is being asked of us?
9. Can a promise be intrinsically wrong to ask in the first place? How so, if yes?
10. Can you make a promise to an animal or to an inanimate object? Why yes or why not?
11. If circumstances change, is it all right to break a promise?

Activities

1. Mark the following example promises as "good to keep," "bad to keep," or not sure. Have the group come up with other test cases.

Promise	Good to make/ keep	Bad to make/ keep	Not sure: explain why
I promise my mother to do my chores			
I promise my coach to be on time for practice			
I promise myself to lose ten pounds in three weeks			

Promise	Good to make/ keep	Bad to make/ keep	Not sure: explain why
I promise my teacher not to cheat on my test			
I promise my friend to not tell on her for smoking			
I promise my dog to take her for a walk every day			
I promise my best friend that I will not tell on her for cheating			

2. On a large sheet of paper or on a board, outline the criteria of what constitutes a promise, including the individual asking it and the person to whom the request to keep the promise is directed. Consider putting up the following categories and having the community fill them in:

- Good promise/bad promise/neutral promise
- Ratings for promises from simple to significant
- Agent requesting the promise/agent making the promise
- Degrees of relationships between them

Exchanges

In this story, the frog asks for an exchange of favors. He will retrieve the princess's golden ball if she will let him eat, drink, and sleep with her. We often engage in exchange transactions. We may promise to do these or not. But let's focus on the concept of transactional exchanges, fairness, and justice. While there was no way that the princess could have dived into the assumingly deep spring and retrieve her ball, this was a relatively easy task for a frog. Was this a fair exchange?

When we exchange goods and services there are two models at work:

- A model of equality: I pay $10 for a doll that is worth $10.
- A model of desire/need: I pay $100 for a doll, which normally sells for $10, but it has a high value in the current market, is scarce, or I do not want to wait for a new shipment.

Immanuel Kant describes this difference when he claims that all items in our experience, with the important exception of rational beings (humans), have a value that is either market value or "fancy value," that is, based on desires and what the market will bear. For Kant, things have price tags but persons are not the kinds of beings that can be so measured. Humans have dignity as self-determining or autonomous (free) agents. This means we cannot set up an exchange between a human being and something of value.

Discussion Questions

1. Did the frog offer a fair exchange to the princess for the retrieval of her golden ball? Why or why not?
2. The toy of the princess was a special golden ball, not just an ordinary rubber one. Since it was very valuable, did that make a difference in what the frog could ask of the princess?
3. He did not ask for stuff or possessions such as the princess offered but friendship. Can you bargain to get a friend?
4. How many types of exchange can you think of? (Some examples: switching lunches, trading clothes, buying a toy; purchasing a meal.)
5. Are there some things or actions that we should not make part of any exchange? For example, would it be OK for someone to exchange their personal freedom if they received enough money for it?

Activities

1. What would have been other exchanges that the frog and princess could have made? That is, the frog could have said, "For me to get your golden ball, you must give me _____. Come up with a number of options and then as a group discuss which one(s) seemed the best and why.
2. Sometimes we can put a monetary value on things; other times there is an emotional value. Pair up with someone in your group; in the following chart, choose which seems appropriate and discuss why:

Items in the exchange or trade	Fair exchange	Unfair exchange	Not sure	Explain your choice
Homework answers for my candy bar				
Money for chores				
A kiss for a date				

Items in the exchange or trade	Fair exchange	Unfair exchange	Not sure	Explain your choice
A slap for a slap				
A full day salary for a half day's work				
A candy bar for an apple				
Make up your own example . . .				

Changing One's Mind

After the princess throws the frog against the wall and he turns into a handsome prince, does she change her mind? Often when we are presented with one set of options, we say 'no' but if the options change, we will agree to the exchange or requests. Is changing your mind a sign of weakness, a refusal to be consistent and stick to your position? Or can changing your mind be justified and even praised? When should we change our mind and when not?

Discussion Questions

1. Did the princess change her mind about the frog when he turned into a prince? Why or why not? Should we praise her for that change?
2. What might be the characteristics or reasons for changing one's mind that would signal this as a good move?
3. Are there characteristics or reasons for changing one's mind that would signal this was not a good move?
4. Can you change your mind about something that you know is true? Why or why not?
5. Could I change my mind but still act the same way or do the same thing?
6. Is changing your mind like lying? How so or how not so?
7. Should the frog have changed his mind about the princess? Why or why not?

Activity

1. Fill in the following chart and discuss with others your results. Make up some of your own examples to discuss.

Example	Good reasons for changing	Bad reasons for changing	Explain each
I was not going to go to the party but I changed my mind and decided to go			
I told my mother I would be home at five but then I decided to stay out until six			
I told my friend that I would loan her my homework but then did not do so			
Tim told Peter that he would play ball with him but then changed his mind and did not show up			

Faithfulness

A seeming add-on to this fairy tale is the character of "Iron Heinrich" whose heart was bound in iron to prevent it from bursting as he was so sad when his master was turned into a frog. When his master returns, the metal bands burst apart from his happiness. Being faithful seems like an important virtue. It is connected to loyalty.

When you first read this tale, it appears to be an odd ending for the prince and his new bride as they ride off to the castle in his magnificent carriage but perhaps there is an important message here. Being faithful could be a theme that runs throughout this story. Is the princess faithful to her promise? Is the frog faithful to the bargain she agreed to? Does the king demand a faithful response from his daughter with regard to her promise?

Discussion Questions

1. Who is the most faithful character in this story? Who is the least?
2. What does it mean to be faithful to
    a. a person,
    b. a promise,
    c. one's self,
    d. what one believes,

e. a pet,
   f. a garden, or
   g. a stranger.
3. Could you lie and be faithful? Tell the truth and not be faithful?
4. Has the princess learned to be more faithful from her experiences? Why yes or why no?

Rewards

Throughout this story we find characters being rewarded or punished for their actions. The frog is rewarded for saving the princess's ball; the princess is first punished for breaking her promise but then is rewarded for keeping it. Sometimes we deserve our reward or punishment but sometimes we do not. In this story, the real question is whether the princess really deserved the reward of a handsome prince and a rich life. The following questions invite the young people to confront the disturbing end to this story.

Discussion Questions

1. Was the princess a nice person? Why or why not?
2. Did she deserve the happy ending?
3. Should the prince be happy with his beautiful princess, given what she did to him?
4. What questions do you have at the end of this fairy tale?

RESOURCES FOR MORE INFORMATION

On frogs: https://defenders.org/frogs/basic-facts.

Tartar, Maria (ed.), *The Annotated Brothers Grimm*. New York: W.W. Norton & Company, 2014.
   This is a lovely collection of the Grimm Fairy Tales with illustrations and margin commentary for the readers. If you would like more information about interpretations of these tales, this is an excellent edition to consult.

Zipes, Jack, *The Original Folk and Fairy Tales of the Brothers Grimm*. Princeton, NJ: Princeton University Press, 2014.
   This edition includes many unfamiliar tales and anecdotes. Many of the Zipes's works in the first edition are violent and include overt sexual overtones; later editions by the grimms changed some of the events within the tales to make them more "child friendly."

Chapter 6

Rapunzel

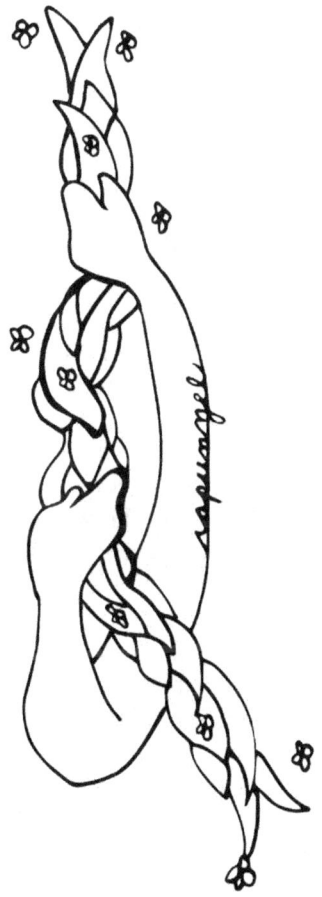

Figure 6.1
Credit Line: Alice V. Gerhardstein

PLOT

The story of Rapunzel is a very familiar one and oft retold in a variety of versions. Some versions depict Rapunzel (or Petrosinella, "Parsley," as Giambattista Basile called her) as quite resourceful and as outsmarting the old woman. Other versions end badly, not true to the happy ending of the typical fairy tale.

The Grimm brothers' version opens with a man and his pregnant wife looking forward to the birth of their baby. The wife, however, gazes out her back window on to a beautiful garden owned by a fairy, later described as an enchantress or often as a witch. She longs for the rapunzel, which turns out to be a kind of lettuce she sees growing there, and begs her husband to get her some.

He sneaks in and steals the lettuce, which his wife eats with great pleasure. She keeps pressuring him to again get her more rapunzel and at first he is reluctant and does not want to trespass to steal the lettuce but she is so insistent and becomes sick that he succumbs out of love for her. However, this time he runs into the fairy who is not pleased about the theft. He explains that his wife was pregnant and wasting away for the delicious rapunzel so the fairy/old woman relents—but extracts a promise from him that he will give her the baby. Desperate on behalf of his wife's health, he agrees.

Curiously, when the baby is born the parents give the girl to the fairy and we hear no more about the parents. The fairy whisks her away and when she turns twelve, she installs the girl in a high tower with only a window and no door. The little girl, Rapunzel, is captive in the tower with no other human contact. One day a prince catches a glimpse of her at a window and becomes entranced. Since he cannot find a way into the tower, he goes away but returns every day.

One day he spies the fairy calling out "Rapunzel, Rapunzel, let down your hair." Two beautiful golden braids are thrown from the window and reach down to the ground and the fairy witch climbs up. After the woman has left, the prince bides his time and then calls out the same phrase. Down come the braids and up climbs the prince. The story is short on details but while initially frightened by the strange man, Rapunzel eventually enjoys his company. We quickly discover what that means.

The version included in the first edition of the Grimm's *Folk and Fairy Tales* recounts how the fairy/witch finds out that Rapunzel has betrayed her when Rapunzel comments how tight her clothes are getting. In the later editions, Rapunzel thoughtlessly comments how much heavier the fairy is than the prince. This shift was most likely made to avoid a covert acknowledgment that Rapunzel is pregnant—hardly an appropriate event in a story for the wholesome family of the late 1800s! Of course, what happens in both versions from then on is fairly familiar.

The fairy is enraged and cuts off Rapunzel's braids and banishes her. When the prince returns to the tower the witch throws down the braids but when he arrives in the window he finds not Rapunzel but a furious witch who promises him he will never see his beloved again. In despair, he throws himself out the window and is blinded. He wanders around the forest and into another land. Eventually he ends up in a hovel where Rapunzel is raising her twin children, a boy and a girl and she recognizes him. Her tears of joy magically restore his sight and yes, they live happily ever after.

TARGETED AGE LEVEL

This story can be clearly read at many levels. For young children, it is a story about a beautiful girl who is hid away, meets her prince, and, ultimately, after challenges, is reunited with him and all ends well.

But many commentaries highlight the sexual narrative behind this story: the young girl is given away at birth, hidden away at the time of puberty, and protected from desirous men. The story continues with a man scaling the tower and impregnating her. Finally she is punished by being outcast because of her sexual betrayal of her guardian. We can also see a disturbing theme of child exchange emerging in the tale and older children and adults may wish to pursue these broader social issues.

READING PLAN

Clearly some of these ideas might be far too scary and adult for your five-year-old. But they will be fascinated by the witch, the tower, and the final happy ending. Given the many versions of this story, read a number of them so as to pick one that you find most appealing and perhaps suitable for your audience.

Regardless of which version you choose to share, teens might be quite interested in the more sophisticated themes: the double standard here of freedom for young men and young women, the question of deception and theft, and the troubling messages of social control of women.

The following discussion plans acknowledge that this story can be read in vastly different ways, and so tailor your engagement with this story as the children or young people direct. Finally, this story offers adults many ideas to pursue, despite its relegation to the realm of "fairy tales for children."

It might be worth noting that the recent film by the Disney corporation, *Tangled*, takes the basic plot but spins it in an entirely different direction. If you are working with teens, a comparison of the ideas in the more traditional version of the story with the movie narrative might be interesting and productive. This suggestion is included at the end of this chapter.

THEMES

Theft

As we see in other fairy tales, characters often steal from others out of greed or desire. In this case, the husband steals the lettuce for his wife out of love and concern for her health. It is worth noting that the wife instigates this entire tragic series of events through her desire for the vegetable. Interestingly enough, we are not told that the couple lacks food, so this is not a case of seeking to meet basic need for sustenance.

Probably most people might have a hard time seeing why anyone would steal rapunzel or any vegetable! But then cravings during pregnancy are often noted. Regardless, the wife in the story claims that she will die without this rapunzel and the husband, out of love for his wife and concern for her well-being, sneaks into the next door garden and steals. So, does he have sufficient reason to steal? Does the fact he is stealing only lettuce affect our view?

We have offered this theme of theft in other chapters as it is a common occurrence in fairy tales but it might generate a different direction in this story.

Discussion Questions

1. In the story, the husband steals from the fairy's garden. In general, is stealing wrong?
2. In this story, suppose that rapunzel grows back when picked, is it still stealing?
3. What if the witch hated lettuce, was it still stealing?
4. Why do you think stealing is wrong, if you think such? Give two reasons.
5. Could there be good reasons to steal? What might those be? For example, a man stealing medicine to save his wife who was dying and that he could not afford? Or is stealing just stealing?
6. Could stealing be a sign of disrespect for another person? Explain your response.

Activity: Create a play

Have the group (two or more children and adults) put the husband on trial for theft and have someone play the husband, another person the witch/old lady, a third the wife, and have someone be the judge. The rest of the class could act as jury. Act out a trial and have each character explain their perspective on the situation. What conclusion do you all reach? Do you think others would agree? Why or why not?

Compromise

In this story, the witch agrees to let the husband have the lettuce as long as he promises to give her the child. She reassures him that the child will be well taken care of.

We often negotiate with others to come to a mutual understanding or to resolve some conflict. The idea is to compromise—for each party to gain but also to give up something that they want.

In many places in life, being able to compromise is vitally important for success and social interaction. But in some cases we do not want to compromise. When is compromise a good solution and when might it be a moral failure?

Discussion Questions

1. The word "compromise" seems to be made of two parts: "com" which means "with" and "promise" which means, well to promise or agree. "Compromise" appears to mean to mutually promise to do something or give up something. How did the fairy/witch and the husband compromise?
2. How can compromising lead to solving conflicts or disagreements?
3. What might be some examples of situations where compromising is the right thing to do?
4. Can you think of some situations where compromising might be the wrong thing?
5. Is compromising the same as giving in?
6. Is compromising the same as giving up?
7. In what way might it be important to develop the "art of compromise"? What do you think that might mean?

The Power of Hair

In the story of *Rapunzel*, the young girl has extremely long hair that allows her to use it as a rope not only for her guardian but also for the prince. When the fairy/witch discovers how Rapunzel betrayed her she cuts off her hair, both to prevent her from helping the prince to climb up the tower and seemingly to punish her. Hair serves as an important cultural signifier throughout history.

In the Judeo-Christian Bible Samson is weakened when Delilah lures him to sleep in her lap and cuts off his hair. Now he no longer has his superhuman strength. While we might not associate hair with strength, we do seem to care a lot about how our hair is styled and how it is perceived by others. Lustrous and long hair is often desired as a biological sign of health.

Most princesses are depicted with long locks and young girls often seek to grow their hair as long as they can. It signals beauty but also femininity for many young women. But how important is hair really? Does it lead us to overemphasize outward appearance?

Discussion Questions

1. Why is Rapunzel's hair so long and how does the story describe it?
2. Who has long hair and what is good about it? Is there anything bad about having long hair?
3. Do all girls have long hair? If not, should they have long hair?
4. Can boys wear their hair long? Why yes or why no?
5. Can you tell what someone is like by looking at their hair? Why yes or why no?
6. If someone colors their hair, are they being deceptive?
7. Why might someone want to change their hair color or texture?

Towers and the Double Standard

In our story, Rapunzel is kept in a tower with no door. Never mind how she got there in the first place, but the concept of a tower is rich in symbolism. When psychologists examine this fairy tale, they often use the tower to express the notion of the social pressure to protect young girls and keep them from sexual experience. When Rapunzel is twelve, she is moved to the tower—the age of puberty. This is interpreted by them to signal the need to protect girls from predatory men.

Guaranteeing paternity was not easy in a pre-DNA culture and men wanted to be assured that the children their wives bore were theirs. The prince, however, is a young man but with no such strictures on his movement. He can travel anywhere he likes. Teens may still see these different treatments in their own families. The boys are allowed more freedom than the girls.

If you are discussing this story with teens, they may wish to focus on the seemingly double standard of freedom for men and women.

Discussion Questions (for Teens and Older)

1. Why do you think Rapunzel was put in the tower when she turned twelve?
2. What might the tower symbolize in this story?

3. Do girls and guys have the same freedom to travel around? Why yes or why no?
4. What role do you think culture plays in the limits we put on the movements of women and men?
5. Is it fair for girls or women to have less freedom of movement than boys or men? Explain your response.
6. Could there be very good reasons to limit the movement of girls rather than that of boys?
7. What criteria should be used to determine what teens can do on their own?

Activity

In the following chart, discuss the cases as fair/not fair and why? Are the boys and girls being treated differently? Are there good reasons for the differences?

Scenario	Fair or not fair	Extenuating circumstances	Criteria used in your judgment
Teen twins (a boy and a girl) are given different curfews			
Your older brother has been in a bit of trouble so your parents ground him but let you go out at night			
Two friends in sophomore year in high school live in the same neighborhood, which is pretty scary at night. One is allowed by her parents to go to her friend's house but not the other			
Megan works at a summer camp and is allowed to accompany the little boys and girls to the bathroom but Jeremy is not			
Gianni can date whomever he wants but his cousin Lucinda is not allowed to date at all, even though she is older			

Parental Responsibility

Rapunzel's parents seem to abscond their responsibility by giving their baby to the fairy/witch in exchange for that lettuce. The fairy tale ignores completely the immensity of this decision and brushes right by it. Should parents ever give their children to others? When do we praise such actions as sacrificial and when do we condemn them as selfish?

This is a difficult and complex theme that might arise with teen and adult readers, but perhaps even young children might wish to explore the motives of Rapunzel's parents in giving her up. If younger children raise this question, tread lightly unless you are equipped with full background knowledge of the children discussing this. You do not want to personalize the conversation about a child in your group.

Discussion Questions (for Young Adults and Adults)

1. Rapunzel's parents seem to quite easily strike a deal in giving up their baby to their neighbor in exchange for lettuce. Could there be good reasons to give up a baby? What might they be, if yes?
2. Are mothers criticized more than fathers if they surrender a baby for adoption? If yes, why might be some reasons? If no, do we differentiate at all in considering this decision?
3. Are there situations where parents should relinquish their baby or children? What parameters might guide this, if yes?
4. Should children themselves have a say in terms of whether they want to stay with their parents? Explain your response.
5. Where should society draw the line between decisions to be made in the privacy of the family and decisions that require outside control or intervention?

Obedience

Rapunzel should obey her parent/guardian but she clearly does not. In our society we hold parental authority as highly important and deserving of respect. But we also acknowledge that there are situations when children are in the right to disobey parents and other adults in their lives.

This can be confusing to young children but perhaps also of great importance to explore. In some situations children should have choices to comply or not. But how do we set those parameters to honor both child and parental authority?

Discussion Questions

1. Does Rapunzel disobey her guardian when she lets the prince visit her?
2. Was it fair that her guardian did not let her have any friends? Why or why not?
3. Should children listen to their parents or guardians? If yes, why?
4. Are there times when children might be able to make their own decisions? If yes, when would that be?
5. How old should a young person be before he or she is able to choose for himself or herself?
6. What criteria mark this change?

Rapunzel and the Movie *Tangled*

Many young children may have seen the Disney movie *Tangled*. You may wish to invite them to compare the two stories. In what ways are the characters alike? What differences do they find? Which story do they like better and why?

Chapter 7

Fitcher's Bird

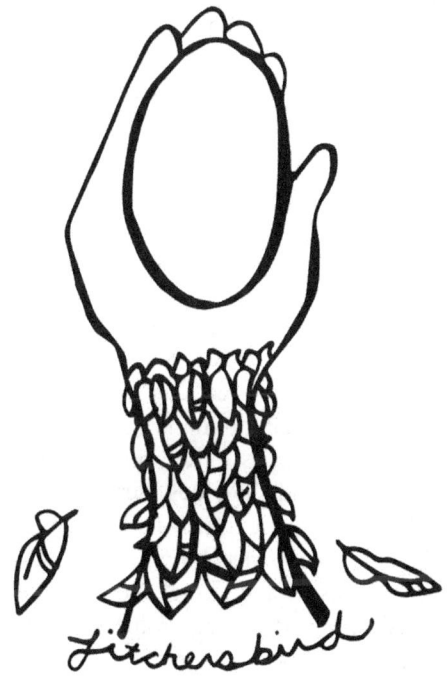

Figure 7.1
Credit Line: Alice V. Gerhardstein

Chapter 7

PLOT

This dark fairy tale offers a version of the *Bluebeard* story. The classic version of *Bluebeard* involves a rich man who marries a series of women, testing each one to see if they will obey him. When they do not, he murders them. Only one woman lives as her brothers come to her rescue and kill Bluebeard. One major difference is that in *Fitcher's Bird* the young woman is resourceful and manages to rescue not only herself but also her two sisters. The story begins with reference to a wizard who is known to take many a young girl away and they are never seen again. He goes to a house where three beautiful girls live, and the oldest answers the door. Merely by touching her he puts her under his spell and she jumps into a basket.

Away he runs and when he gets to his beautiful house full of riches, he promises her anything. She seems fine with this until one day he says he is going away and she can go into any room in the house that she chooses but one. He also gives her a key and an egg, which he demands that she carry around. Of course, she ends up going into the forbidden room and discovers to her horror a basin of blood full of body parts. In her fright she drops the egg in the bowl but immediately retrieves it.

Alas, no matter how she tries to wipe off the blood, the stain remains. When the wizard returns he asks for the egg and realizes that she disobeyed him. He drags her to the bloody room and to her death and dismemberment. This whole scenario is repeated with the second daughter.

When he returns for the third one, the youngest, she is justifiably suspicious. This girl likewise explores all the rooms but she puts the egg in a safe place so that when she enters the bloody room, her horror at recognizing both her sisters' bodies in pieces does not lead her to drop the egg. She has, however, learned that this is not the guy to marry.

She successfully collects the parts of her sisters and magically puts them back together. They embrace and she hides them in another room. When he returns she gives back the pristine egg and he believes he has found a bride true and obedient. She promises to marry him but insists that he deliver a basket full of gold to her parents. In the basket she hides her sisters and covers them with gold and tells them to send their brothers back to rescue her. She orders the wizard to hasten to her family home with no stopping along the way.

At this point she has the upper hand and he appears to have to obey her. On the way he notes how heavy the basket is but when he thinks about putting it down, one of the sisters, pretending to be the intended bride, cries out to keep moving and that she is watching from a tower. Meanwhile the bride-to-be has invited all of the wizard's friends to the house for the wedding and has placed a grinning skull decorated with flowers and jewels in an attic room to mimic her presence.

As the wizard travels home he sees what he takes to be his bride in the upper window and waves. Our heroine has rolled herself in honey and covered herself with feathers, then proceeds to dance her way through the forest passing the unsuspecting wizard as she sings a song about being Fitcher's bird. When the wizard arrives home all the guests are inside the house but her brothers have followed and they set fire to the house which goes up in a blaze, killing the wizard and all. Justice is achieved. Here we have one of the darker fairy tales, despite the seemingly happy ending.

TARGETED AGE LEVELS

This rather gruesome story may be better shared with older children and teens. Adults will be familiar with the Bluebeard legend and will most likely catch the parallels. The Grimm's collection includes a version of *Bluebeard* as well. Children can be fascinated by blood and gore and most likely their reading of this story will focus on the magic and the third sister who saves the day. The themes below can be chosen for discussion based on your audience and their age and interest in raising questions and concerns.

READING PLAN

What makes *Fitcher's Bird* particularly noteworthy is the ingenuity of the third sister who actually rescues her sisters and herself, even if the brothers are tasked with killing the evil wizard in the end. This fairy tale has been interpreted through a psychoanalytical lens with a focus on the egg symbolizing chastity and the cynical belief that women cannot be trusted. Men have to tear them away from their family through trickery and then jealously safeguard their "possession" so as to protect their own interests. Older readers may wish to compare the more familiar *Bluebeard* story with this one.

One technique in reading for philosophical inquiry is to pause every now and then and have the participants assess what concepts or actions seem worthy of pursing in dialogue. Sometimes a word itself can generate a rich philosophical discussion. The motives of the characters, while never made explicit, may also come up for question.

As always, these stories can be read at many different levels and can lead to discussions in a myriad of directions. Be willing to follow where the participants wish to go and do not feel compelled to direct them toward particular themes.

THEMES TO EXPLORE

Danger

This story is replete with danger. Girls go off with strangers and are never heard from again. They are threatened, terrorized, and killed. Danger seems to lurk in every corner of this dark tale. What constitutes danger and how can we recognize it? Do some of the characters bring it upon themselves? Does that change the nature of the danger?

Discussion Questions

1. What dangers do we find in this story? List them.
2. Are strangers dangerous? Why yes or no?
3. Are dangers always caused by people?
4. Try to describe the criteria that would make any situation dangerous.
   Hint: an event, situation, person that leads to uncertainty, possible harm, the feeling of uncontrol, apprehension of the future, lack of confidence, novelty that seems too novel or different, and so on.
5. Can dangers be exciting and fun? Give examples.
6. Can danger be advantageous or good for us? Give reasons.

Activity

In the following chart, indicate which event/individual/situation is dangerous and what criteria you used. Add your own examples and ask others to respond.

Example	Dangerous? Yes or no	Criteria used	Good danger or bad?	Reasons for choice
A bee flies in your window				
You are riding with your dad and the brakes in the car fail				
Your best friend decides to play with someone else				
A huge snowstorm hits your town				

Example	Dangerous? Yes or no	Criteria used	Good danger or bad?	Reasons for choice
You visit New York City and take the subway				
You walk by a neighbor's house and their dog barks at you				
You attempt a dive from the high board at the pool				

Fear

There are many scenes in this fairy tale that are very scary, both for the characters in the story and for the readers. Fear is unpleasant and we generally try to avoid situations where we become fearful, much as we do danger. We could see fear as a reasonable reaction to danger. Danger is the catalyst and fear is the response.

Children are often fearful of the dark, of certain animals, or of displeasing their parents or teachers. But older young people and adults also experience fear. And while danger may elicit this emotion, many other situations can do so likewise. We encounter fear of public speaking, fear of being wrong, and, in some situations, fear of the unknown. But we might also see where fear is a good thing to experience.

Discussion Questions

1. There are many fearful moments in this story. Which part of the story do you think is the most fearful for the characters? For you the reader/the listener?
2. Can you give examples of things or situations where you were scared or fearful? Briefly describe the situation.
3. Can you pick out the qualities or aspects of the situation that made you scared or fearful? Make a list and if you are discussing this with others, compare.
4. Fear seems to be a feeling that is accompanied by some awareness or knowledge and often by imagination. How do these work to bring about fear?
5. What is the difference between being scared watching a spooky movie, being scared on a roller coaster or carnival ride, and being scared to walk alone into an empty house?
6. While we tend to think of being scared or fearful as a negative feeling to be avoided, could having fear be a good experience? Why yes or why no?

Activity

Choose the scenarios contributed by your child or group for 2 above, write them on a board or on a big pad of paper and have everyone discuss (a) is the fear a good kind or bad and (b) why and how someone could get over their fear in the particular situation.

Strangers

Many fairy tales include implicit or explicit warnings about strangers. Often these people live away from the community, in the woods, or some other isolated place. In some cases the strangers come to the home of the main characters and offer them something or request something. Interestingly enough, much as in the tradition of the bible and mythology, the people welcome the stranger. Perhaps it is an angel or god in disguise?

In this story, the wizard goes to the houses where young marriage-aged girls live and magically captures them. As in many such tales, instead of word-spreading and caution-building, it continues to happen. In the original *Bluebeard* story the man is wealthy and that seems to overcome a lot of scruples on the part of parents. But the continued disappearance of one daughter after the other should certainly raise suspicions!

We are in fairyland and those doses of reality tend not to apply. But in our society today "stranger danger" is a common mantra, despite the fact that most crimes against children are committed by those with whom they are familiar. But who is the stranger and how can we walk the line between being careless about our safety and being indifferent and outright hostile to those we do not know? This is a big theme to explore in some depth with children and adults.

Discussion Questions

1. The wizard visits houses where he is a stranger to the inhabitants. What makes someone a stranger?
2. Is being a stranger the same as being strange? Why yes or why no?
3. Depending where you live, you might see strangers all the time or hardly ever. Share whether you encounter any strangers in your community. What makes them strangers to you?
4. Can someone become a friend from being a stranger? If yes, how so?
5. How should we treat strangers?
6. Does it matter how old they are? How old you are? In what ways yes or no?
7. Are strangers bad, good, both, or neither? Explain.

Activity

Fill out the following chart as a group and discuss your answers. You can elaborate on the scenarios, perhaps even coming to different conclusions based on details you provide. Come up with your own examples.

A stranger . . .	Good or bad stranger? [you may need to elaborate on the context]	Why did you choose your response?	What you should say or do	Comments
Smiles at you while you are in a grocery store line				
Offers you some candy or money				
Asks for directions to a gas station				
Asks you where you live				
Calls after you that you dropped your hat				
Cheers the winning team at a baseball game				
Asks for your help				

Curiosity

One of the messages in this story is the danger brought on by the curiosity of the women who are told not to enter a certain room but seem driven to disobey and peek. This goes back to the myth of Pandora's box or Eve in the Garden. However, we human beings are all curious. And children especially so when told not to do something. What drives curiosity? Is it a strength or weakness? And is this something that girls and women are particularly prone to? Perhaps we need more curiosity in ourselves?

Discussion Questions

1. The wizard tests each girl by telling her not to go in a certain room. What do you think his reasons are for doing this and what reasons might each woman have had for not following his orders?
2. What are you curious about? Write a list and explain.
3. Are kids more curious than adults? Girls more than boys? Why yes or no?
4. There is an old saying, "Curiosity killed the cat and satisfaction brought it back." What does that mean?
5. Is curiosity helpful in school? If yes, how so, and if no, why not?
6. Where else does curiosity help us?
7. Can curiosity hurt us or be a negative force in our lives? How so, if yes?
8. If you are no longer curious, is that a good thing?

Activities

1. Create a list of words that you think connect to curiosity. Include nouns and verbs. Make a "word cloud" on paper or a board. Discuss.
2. See if you can find out who invented each of the following. Discuss what the inventors were curious about that drove them to their inventions:

The wheel	_____
Growing vegetables	_____
The telephone	_____
Vaccines	_____
Anesthesia	_____
Computers	_____
Movies	_____
Windmills	_____
Video games	_____

Evil

Fitcher's Bird features a very evil protagonist who seemingly kills young women without a second thought. The dismemberment adds an even more intense note of evil in this disturbing story. We are given no reason as to why the wizard is such a bad actor in the tale but in the end he, and all his friends, are burned alive by the avenging brothers.

Fairy tales often feature bad people and usually they get their comeuppance in the end. Justice is served. But evil is a troubling and complex concept. Psychologists attempt to explain actions that appear deeply evil based on abusive upbringing or even biological causes. We want evil to be punished at the end of a story and if it is not, we are left deeply distressed and dissatisfied.

Discussion Questions

1. Is the wizard a bad person or does he act in bad ways? Explain.
2. What makes a person bad or evil? Can you list characteristics that you would say all bad people share? (See the following activity to help you.)
3. Could someone act badly but not be bad? How so or why not?
4. Could someone act nicely but still be a bad person? Why yes or no?
5. Is being bad the same as being evil?
6. Are you bad if you only do one thing that is bad?
7. Can bad people become good people?
8. If you have friends who are bad, does that make you bad?

Activity 1

Invite each child or young person to write a short essay or draw a picture about a time when they did something bad. Who thought it was bad? Did their act make them a bad person? Do you have to do something when you acted badly not to be a bad person? If they are comfortable sharing, have them read their essay or share their picture with the others and discuss. However, if this makes anyone uncomfortable be open to making this optional or have them write a fictionalized story.

Activity 2

Use this exercise to help you build a list of criteria for being bad or being evil. Fill in the following chart and discuss your choices. Can you add any options to the chart?

Are you bad if you . . .	Yes or no	Reasons for your choice
Wish someone ill		
Intend to hurt someone but do not		
Hurt someone but did not intend to		
Did not help someone who needed help and asked you		
Wished that someone would suffer		
Laugh at someone who is crying		
Feel bad about someone who is happy or successful		
Refuse to let your younger brother play your guitar		

Activity 3

When fairy tales are illustrated, the good and bad people in the stories are usually depicted in ways that leave you no doubt which is which. Explore some illustrations of *Fitcher's Bird* and compare the way in which the various characters are presented. What can you conclude about visualizations of fairy tale characters?

Chapter 8

Little Red Riding Hood

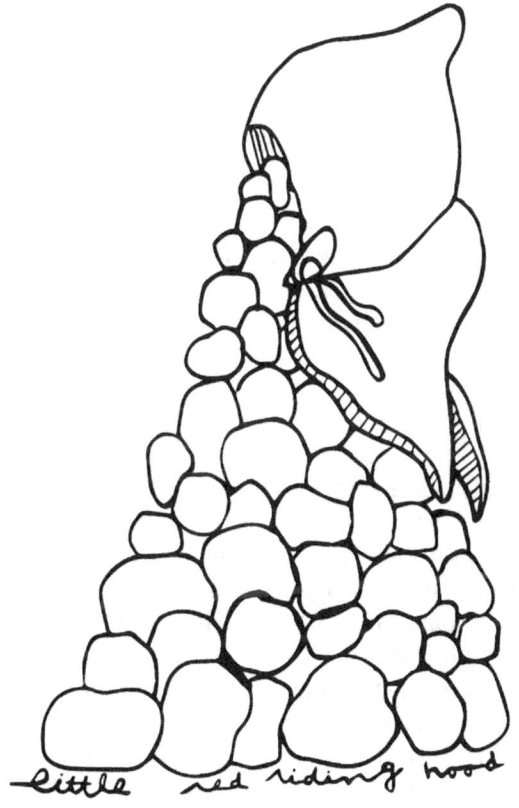

Figure 8.1
Credit Line: Alice V. Gerhardstein

PLOT

This fairy tale is one of the most popular tales for children and offers a field day for psychologists and sociologists to dissect for layers of meaning. It has been mined for theories of gender, social practice, concepts of male/female, nature/culture, and childhood anxieties—the list is endless. It has also been presented in many different forms over the centuries. The early oral versions were quite bawdy and sexualized, while the familiar versions from our childhood are scary but far more suitable for the young.

The Grimm brothers' version opens with introducing a "dear little girl" whose grandmother made her a red velvet hood. She loved it so much she wore it all the time and hence gained her nickname. One day her mother sends her into the forest to visit her grandmother who is ailing. Charged with bringing cakes and wine and told to stay to the path and not dawdle, Little Red Riding Hood takes off but soon meets a wolf.

She greets him politely and, upon being asked, tells him where she is going. The wolf thinks to himself that this looks to be a tasty treat and he can also eat up her grandmother if he gets there first. As he walks next to her he suggests she look round and perhaps enjoy the lovely woods. Spying some flowers, the girl decides to follow his advice and pick a lovely bouquet for her grandmother.

Of course, the wolf sprints ahead, walks in on grandmother and gobbles her up. He then climbs into her bed and waits. Meanwhile our heroine, after picking many flowers, realizes she is behind time and scampers off to her grandmother's. Although noting the door is open, she goes in and enters her grandmother's bedroom. Here she has the familiar exchange on how big are her grandmother's ears, eyes, hands, and finally teeth. The wolf jumps out of bed and devours her, promptly falling into a deep sleep, and snores.

A passing huntsman hears the weird sounds (the wolf snoring) and fortuitously enters in to discover the said wolf. Instead of shooting him, he surmises that the wolf may have eaten the old lady and grabbing a pair of scissors he cuts the wolf open and out jump the girl, followed by her grandmother, whole and sound. They fill the wolf's cavity with rocks and when he wakes up he falls down and dies.

There is a short coda to this tale where Little Red Riding Hood meets the wolf again as she travels to her grandmother's but this time she is smart and rushes ahead to alert her. They lock themselves in the house and ultimately lure the wolf, who climbed on their roof, to his death by drowning in a trough which was full of water from cooking sausages. "Little Red Riding Hood walked home cheerfully, and no one ever did her any harm."

The version by Charles Perrault cautions listeners that young ladies should heed the advice to beware of wolves as there are many of them who walk upright and look like decent young men—a cautionary ending indeed.

TARGETED AGE LEVEL

This wonderful story invites all sorts of inquiry: from little children up through adults. From the following themes, choose the ones that support the reactions from your child, teen, or your adult group. You can adjust some of the suggested questions to fit your audience. And as always, be alert to new themes not included here. Your young people may follow a path of inquiry that may completely surprise you. Follow their lead and see where their conversation takes them.

READING PLAN

Most children, and certainly teens and adults, are familiar with the story but it always benefits from a fresh reading. One approach might be to ask your partner or group to pick out words that interested or puzzled them. What does Little Red Riding Hood look like? The wolf? Follow the query where it takes you. They may be familiar with a different version so ask them if they find any major differences. The familiarity of this tale lends itself to some fun explorations and twists.

THEMES TO EXPLORE

Wolves

A prominent character in this tale is, of course, the wolf. Wolves tend to get a bad rap; they tend to be solitary animals who are devoted to their pack. But in past centuries where the economy depended upon domesticated herds of animals like cows or sheep, wolves could be a real menace. They also represented a wild nature that was not kind or caring. This is nature as the Other and as such, it menaces humans and their society. For most of human history, humankind has struggled against the forces of nature to survive, and predators like wolves were just one of many challenges they faced.

Our contemporary urban existence tends to romanticize animals and nature in ways which those who live in less developed areas find naïve. But perhaps this tale might introduce an opportunity to learn more about a maligned species, one which seems to be a distant relative of "man's best friend," the dog.

Discussion Questions

1. This tale features the big bad wolf. What makes a wolf the villain in so many stories?
2. If wolves were known to be dangerous, why did Little Red Riding Hood engage in conversation with this one?
3. The wolf in this story seems to be quite humanized; it speaks with Little Red Riding Hood and acts in ways that seem predatory in a very human way. What else might the wolf represent in this story?
4. If the wolf is simply acting like a wolf, does the wolf deserve his final punishment? Why yes or why no?

Activity

What do you know about wolves? Are they similar to domesticated dogs? How so and perhaps how are they different? Do different species of wolves live and behave differently? As a project, investigate wolf behavior and create a poster that summarizes your findings.

Trust

In this story we find Little Red Riding Hood to be naïvely trustful of the wolf. But her mother is also trustful of her in sending her out to visit her grandmother on her own. How do we decide whom we can trust? Do you choose who to trust based on their age? Where does trust factor into our daily lives?

Children are often completely trustful of their parents and indeed, we might think that trust is essential in good parenting. As they venture out into the world they learn that not everyone can be trusted. And perhaps not trusting someone is equally important to trusting others. But trust can also be seen as a virtue and a positive aspect of human nature.

Discussion Questions

1. Who in this story shows trust in another person? Describe how they show their trust.
2. Who in your life do you think is worthy of trust? Why?
3. Can you trust only people? What about animals? Can you trust your house, bike, the sun? Why yes or why no?
4. What do you need to place trust in someone? Try listing the characteristics of those people or other beings that you trust.

5. Is having trust a good thing? Why? Could being trustful not be so good?
6. Are there individuals we must trust? If yes, who, when, and why?

Activity: Charting Trust

In the following chart, indicate which persons or beings we ought to trust and why. Compare your answers with others and discuss why you chose as you did. You might wish to come up with some other examples to see what others think.

Example	We should trust	We should not trust	Reasons for your choice
Your parents			
Your siblings			
A teacher			
A police officer			
A librarian			
A dog you meet in the park			
Your friends			
The president of the country			
Your school bus driver			

Learning a Lesson

The tale of *Little Red Riding Hood* seems to be a cautionary tale with our heroine being punished but then saved and all ends well. Her mother clearly gives her instructions on what she is to do and chatting with wolves and straying off the path to grandmother's house are not on the list. Children and young people reading this may clearly get that message. Older readers may see the sexual overtones hinted at in the Grimm's version but not as explicitly as in the earlier ones.

When we do not listen to the sound advice of our parents or others in authority, bad things can happen and while LRRH appears to be quite young in our tale, we can easily imagine the teenager who rebels against the advice of her family to watch out for those "wolves." Depending on your audience you may wish to explore the cautionary messages here in quite different directions.

Discussion Questions

1. Was Little Red Riding Hood a bad girl for not obeying her mother? Give reasons for your response.
2. Did she learn a lesson from her experience? What lesson was that?
3. Do you think that her mother would have given the same warning to her brother?

4. Is there an easy and hard way to learn a lesson? Share your responses here and discuss.
5. Is learning a lesson the same as going to school? Why yes or why no?

Activity: Learning a Lesson

Fill out the following chart and discuss your answers with others. Try creating your own examples and see what others say.

	Did the person "learn their lesson"?		
Sample event	Yes—explain	No—explain	Comments
Mary tries to pet a dog in the park and he growls at her			
Tim tackles a hard math problem and figures out how to solve it			
John spray-paints a fence with graffiti and no one ever finds out it was him			
When the clerk at the store gives too much change, Patrick returns the extra amount			
Teresa forgets to study for the history test and does very poorly but her mother rewards her with an ice cream cone for trying			

Kindness

Our heroine shows kindness. She happily takes a treat to visit her sick grandmother and she is quite polite to the wolf. Some would say that kindness is the ultimate virtue. But can kindness veer into carelessness or get one in danger?

Kindness implies trust as one reaches out to be nice to someone, assuming that they will respond in kind. But should we strive to be kind, regardless of the response we receive? Or is being kind important in its own right, regardless of the response?

Discussion Questions

1. Little Red Riding Hood acts kindly in this story. She willingly ventures out to bring her grandmother some treats and she treats the wolf with respect and even kindness. What are some examples of being kind from your own experiences?
2. If someone treats us kindly, should we respond with kindness back?
3. What if someone treats us badly or in a mean way? Should we still be kind toward them? Why yes or why not?
4. Kindness can be demonstrated in things we do, what we say, and even what we think. Offer some examples of each type. Are there other ways to be kind?
5. What does it mean to be kind to yourself?
6. Could we be kind but also be deceptive at the same time? Would this be OK? Why or why not? Offer a story or scenario to illustrate your response.

Strangers

Many fairy tales introduce the idea of dealing with strangers. Sometimes they turn out to be benevolent, like fairy godmothers, but other times they can be wicked witches in disguise, like in *Hansel and Gretel*. Children are often cautioned not to talk to strangers and certainly not to go off with them.

But could a stranger be simply a friend we do not yet know? And do we tend to see people who are different from us as strangers and as individuals with whom we cannot and should not associate? How do we caution young people to deal with strangers in ways which do not endanger them but also do not scare them away from others?

We explore this theme in the chapter on *Fitcher's Bird*, but it might be worth revisiting here. If we are too fearful of strangers or reluctant to accept them, we might lose out on new relationships. The suspicion of strangers can also be at the core of prejudice.

Discussion Questions

1. Is the wolf a stranger to Little Red Riding Hood or does she seem to already know him?
2. Try to describe the steps one takes from strangers meeting to becoming good friends.
3. Should I be kind to a stranger? Why yes or why no?
4. Why does the huntsman seem to be willing to help out the grandmother, a stranger?
5. Should children and adults treat strangers differently? Explain your answer.

6. Why do we tell children to avoid strangers?
7. Is being strange the same as being a stranger?
8. How different or unknown does a person or creature have to be to be a stranger?

Activity

Complete the following sentence and write it on an index card. Then spread them out on a table and see what connections there are among them. Discuss your responses.

A Stranger is someone who _____.

Chapter 9

The White Snake

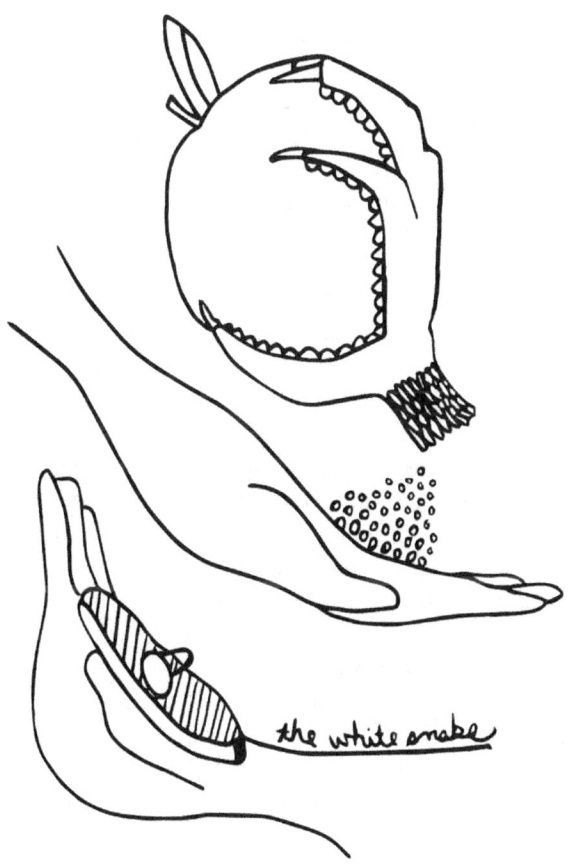

Figure 9.1
Credit Line: Alice V. Gerhardstein

Chapter 9

PLOT

This wonderful tale introduces us to a resourceful servant whose curiosity leads him to take a bite of the king's secret meal. This act of transgression gives him the power to understand the language of animals and we see a curious vacillation from appreciating and helping animals to using them for human purposes.

A king is noted for his incredible wisdom and no one knows his secret. Every day his servant brings him a special covered plate, the contents of which he consumes in private. One day the curious servant sneaks the platter into his own room and opens it to find a white snake. He is possessed by a desire to taste it and takes one bite, which magically gives him the power to understand the language of animals.

Soon after the queen loses a precious ring and as the servant has free range of the castle, the king promptly blames him. Unless he can find the ring and the culprit by morning, he will be executed. As he wonders what will become of him, he overhears two ducks chatting and one complains of a stomachache caused by eating a ring. He grabs the duck, takes it to the cook, and upon slaughtering it, they find the ring. The king promises him any job he would like but the servant asks for a horse and some money for a journey. Off he goes.

On his way he demonstrates kindness to three types of creatures. He frees some struggling fish from the reeds when he hears them bemoaning their fate; he moves his horse off the road when he overhears an ant king complaining that his people are being trampled; and he rescues three baby ravens whose parents have kicked them out of the nest. Our young man kills his horse so that the baby ravens won't starve! He walks on and comes to a kingdom where the princess is looking for a husband. Each candidate must pass a test and if he fails then the young suitor is executed.

Upon seeing the princess, the young man falls in love and is determined to win her hand. The king takes him to the ocean and throws a ring into the deep. If he can get the ring back from the bottom of the ocean by morning, he can marry her. What to do? As he sits on the shore, the three fishes he has saved swim up with the ring. However, when he brings the ring to the princess she is not welcoming.

She is not happy to have a commoner solve the challenge and she orders another trial. She has ten sacks of grain dumped in the garden and commands him to pick up every grain by morning or else.... Again, the young man is sure he will lose but in the morning the grain has been neatly returned to the sacks, thanks to the hardworking ants who came to his rescue in gratitude for his willingness to move off the path.

For the third and final trial, the proud princess demands that he bring him an apple from the "tree of life." This might be a reference to the biblical tree in the Garden of Eden but our young hero has no idea where even to begin. He wanders out through three kingdoms and is about ready to give up when a golden apple falls in his lap. Three ravens land and proclaim that they are the grownup chicks he saved from starvation. They heard of his plight and flew across the earth to fetch the golden apple.

The princess is amazed by his success and has run out of excuses. As each takes a bite of the apple, they fall in love and lived happily ever after.

READING PLAN

This fairy tale may be unfamiliar to your audience but it offers enchanting opportunities to explore ideas about language, humans and animals, and favors. In addition to the mythic theme of learning the language of other animals, we find here the pairing up of three good deeds done out of kindness with the three trials and how those very animals pay back the assistance they received.

There are so many different directions this tale can go with your group or child so be prepared to follow their lead. As always, open up the conversation with what interested them, surprised them, annoyed them. What questions do they have? If one of the themes below seems relevant, try the questions but be willing to follow their lead. The fact that this tale may be unknown to your audience might generate some new ideas!

THEMES TO EXPLORE

Wisdom and Knowledge

The tale opens with the introduction of a king so known for his wisdom that it appeared as if he knew everything, as if "the winds must be carrying news to him." What is the difference between knowledge and wisdom? Wisdom and being smart or intelligent? We sometimes assume that wisdom comes with age and experience but we can also clearly see that does not always happen. But can a very young child be wise? Philosophers have always valued wisdom but determining precisely its nature is challenging. Interestingly enough, the tale moves past this opening part of the story quickly but discussing knowledge and wisdom is well worthwhile.

Discussion Questions

1. The king is famous for being wise. How can you tell if a person is wise?
2. In this tale, what does wisdom seem to mean?

3. Is wisdom the same as knowledge? Why or why not?
4. Does being wise mean one has all the answers?
5. Does being wise mean one has all the questions?
6. Is wisdom something one has or something one does? Both? Neither?

Roundtable Activity

If you have a group of children or young people, ask them to see if they can name a person that they know of who is wise. Each respondent should frame their answer in this way:

_____ is wise because he or she _____.

After everyone has shared their example, see if the group can find any important common elements or different ones.

Language

Many myths and legends reference the precious ability to understand other animals as a wonderful skill to possess. In Norse mythology, Siegfried tastes dragon's blood and can understand the birds. Harry Potter of far more recent fame can speak and understand the language of serpents, "Parseltongue." In this fairy tale the king eats a white snake, which allows him access to the secret world of animal communications.

The young man likewise acquires the ability to understand animals after only one small taste. Of course, we know that many animals do communicate, if not with language similar in structure to ours, through all sorts of means.

Discussion Questions

1. How many different animals can the young man understand in this tale?
2. Many cartoons and movies like to depict animals speaking our language. Why do you think they do that?
3. How do we use language? Do babies and young children use language the same way as older children and adults? Explain your answer.
4. Can we communicate with someone who does not speak or understand our language and we cannot speak or understand theirs? How so, if yes?
5. Try to communicate with a partner but do not use words! Were you able to be understood? How so?
6. What does the phrase "body language" mean? Are there things you can communicate only with spoken or written language?

Activity

Clearly, animals can communicate to one another, at least within species and sometimes across species. Pick an animal from the following list and find out how the animal communicates. But how would we know that animals were communicating? Look to see if you can find this out as well.

Giraffes	Snakes	Flies
Apes	Bees	Deer
Dogs	Butterflies	Raccoons
Cats	Ants	Cows
Fish	Bats	Pigs
Whales	Lions	Chickens
Dolphins Rats	Elephants	

Blame

In this tale, the king is quick to blame his servant for the theft of the ring. This seems odd coming from someone supposedly so wise. How can we best determine responsibility for mistakes or crimes? Was there enough evidence to hold the servant as potentially guilty, even if it turned out that he was indeed innocent? To blame someone can imply that they had a choice to do or not do the offending act. But might we also lay the blame on someone or something even if there is no direct responsibility? Does blame mean the same thing in these cases?

Discussion Questions

1. Why did the king blame the servant for the missing ring? What evidence did he have?
2. Would a wise person do this?
3. Would a knowledgeable person come to this conclusion?
4. What does it mean to blame someone for some action, event, or situation?
5. Are there situations where no one is to blame? What might they be?
6. Can we blame someone for an action they could not avoid?
7. If you are blamed for something, what should you do? Create a scenario to illustrate your response.

Kindness II

Many fairy tales introduce kindness as a sign of character. But this story offers some strange behaviors on the part of the servant. On the one hand, when he can understand the language of animals, he responds with great compassion and comes to their assistance. But he also thinks nothing of turning the duck over to the cook to slaughter and resorts to killing his own horse so that the baby ravens might eat. So, has he learned compassion for fellow creatures through his ability to understand them or only a selective care? And why some animals but not others?

Are some animals worth more sympathy and care than others? And yet his kindness is significantly rewarded by the three types of animals that come to his aid when he needs it: animals of the sea, the earth, and the air. This story follows the fairy tale trope where the hero or heroine is ultimately rewarded for kindness shown to others.

Discussion Questions

1. The servant shows three acts of genuine kindness toward animals in distress. What are they?
2. But he also shows some actions of almost cruelty toward animals. Can you find those in this tale? Was he being cruel, or did he have justified reasons for his actions?
3. What does it mean to be kind?
4. Is being kind a feeling we have, something we do, something we say?
5. Should you be kind to something or someone who hurt you?
6. If someone is kind to you, do you owe them kindness in return?
7. Is being kind a type of bargain? If X is kind to Y, then Y must do something kind for X in return?
8. How does acting kind affect others? Affect one's self?

Animals and People

As we have explored earlier this tale offers us a chance to think about our relationship to animals, as well as to other people. Much has been written about how we humans have treated animals very poorly. But many animals depend on humans for their existence and some would not exist at all if humans did not use them. How ought we to relate to other species? It might be easy to say that we should respect and love all animals but some of them are quite dangerous to humans and others want nothing to do with us.

Children and animals often go together in one's imagination. How many children grow up with stories featuring animals and soft toy animals to hug? Their pets might be quite precious to them. Depending upon the children with whom you are sharing this story, you might engage in a discussion about the value of pets, whether we should eat meat or use animal products, and how we might depend on those animal products for our own health and well-being.

The following questions and activities will work with very different situations, so choose which ones seem more meaningful to your children or young people.

Discussion Questions

1. In this tale we see the servant helping animals who in turn help him when he needs it and their skill sets work far better than his. Which of the three types of animals did you feel the most sympathy for and why?
2. What do we owe animals and does that vary among different types of animals? Consider mammals, insects, fish, and birds.
3. What about what we might owe animals based on where they live? For example, consider pets, farm animals, animals that live in your yard, animals that live in the wild.
4. In the tale, the young man helps some animals but sacrifices others. Are some types of animals due more care and respect than others? What criteria would we use if we want to make distinctions?

Activity

In the following chart decide whether the animal would be a pet or not. Explain your answers to others in your group and discuss. Add some animals to see what others think.

Animal	Good as a pet	OK to eat	Not OK to eat	Reasons for your choices
Dogs				
Parakeets				
Chickens				
Cows				
Goldfish				
Cats				
Rats				
Crickets				
Pandas				
Foxes				
Pigs				

Animal	Good as a pet	OK to eat	Not OK to eat	Reasons for your choices
Falcons				
Turkeys				
Lions				

Challenges, Trials, and Fairness

The princess and her father set a series of challenges for the young man to meet. It might seem that they get increasingly harder to do. After the young man fulfills the first one by getting the ring from the depths of the ocean, the princess insists on more trials because she thinks he is not important enough to marry her; that is, he is not in her social caste. Was she being unfair here?

The previous suitors who failed the first challenge were executed. Is that a fair punishment for their failure? It seems we find in this tale a web of trials, promises, and broken promises. Is it fair to up the ante if a trial is completed but we do not like the results? In short, is there something wrong with the princess's attitude here?

Discussion Questions

1. It seems that the princess changes the rules of the "game" each time the young man meets the challenge. What reason does she have? Is this a good reason?
2. Since the princess and her father created the challenges, is this fair that they keep adding new ones?
3. How would you define "fairness"? In games? In a family setting? In school?
4. Are the rules of a game the same as a promise? Why yes or why no?
5. In the end the young man and princess get married. Do you think he did the right thing? Why yes or why do you think he did not?

Chapter 10

The Little Mermaid

Figure 10.1
Credit Line: Alice V. Gerhardstein

PLOT

Unlike many other fairy tales in this book, *The Little Mermaid* was composed by a single individual, Hans Christian Andersen. Andersen includes many Christian references within his story. The story is familiar to many children today through the popular Disney movie version but the original story is far darker and richer in descriptions but oddly with much less violence and fighting than the Disney version. One of the attractive elements of this fairy tale is the close detailed descriptions of the ocean sea, its creatures, and the beauty of the natural world. Detailed visual imagery suffuses the story and offers the readers wondrous images, full of color and light.

The story opens with the six young mermaids living with the sea king and his own mother who looks after the young mermaids. Andersen describes how they live amid the sway sea forests, and deep blue ever-moving waves. When each mermaid turns fifteen, she is allowed to rise to the surface to see the world above. Year by year, each one gets a chance to rise up and see what the above-sea world is like and they come back down to recount their visions to the others.

The youngest mermaid is enthralled by the outside world and is impatient to experience it herself. When her turn comes, she is entranced by the beauty around her and ends up spying on a ship out on the water to celebrate the prince's sixteenth birthday. When a violent storm comes up the ship capsizes and she rescues the young prince, bringing him back to land and watching over him until some young girls run up to find him.

Now she longs to live among humans and wants to be with the handsome prince. Her grandmother chides her and reminds her that mermaids live for 300 years but then become sea foam and vanish while humans have immortal souls and after death continue to exist. Mermaids and humans are too different from one another. But she is determined.

She visits the sea witch whose dark and scary kingdom is described in gruesome imagery. The little mermaid trades her voice for a special drug that will split her tail into two legs but the sea witch warns her that walking on those legs will be like walking on daggers with extraordinary pain. The sea witch further warns her that unless the prince loves her truly and marries her before God, she will die and turn into sea foam. She will never be able to return to her mermaid form. Nevertheless, she agrees and ends up on the shore near the castle, drinks the potion, and wakes up in great pain but with two legs.

Of course, the prince finds her and brings her home, but he treats her rather like a favored pet, enjoying her company. Remember, she cannot speak or make a sound. She dresses like a page and follows him on his hunts and expeditions. The mermaid treasures the adventures and all that she gets to explore but she remains deeply in love with the prince who is clearly fond of her but not in any way romantically. When he has to visit a neighboring country to meet a possible bride, she accompanies him and he assures her that he would rather play with her. But instead he falls immediately in love with his intended and they decide to get married.

The wedding is on a boat and is lusciously described in all its beauty. The mermaid can only dance, magically and beautifully—but with great pain—on her two legs. However, at night, her sisters rise up from the sea. They had all sacrificed their long flowing hair to the sea witch to get a magic dagger that if our mermaid plunges into the young prince will magically restore her to her mermaid self and she will be able to return to the sea. But she cannot do it.

She flings the dagger out to sea and transforms into . . . not sea foam but a spirit being of the air. Air spirits crowd around her and promise that she too can have eternal life after 300 years of good deeds. Of course, if they visit the homes with children and those children are being good, well, the spirits get good points for that! Ah, but if the children are misbehaving, they have days added to the time they must wait for redemption.

We do not find the clear-cut romantic "live happily ever after" that the movie version offers us and there are no adorable little sea creatures for comic relief. Instead, we find a tragic tale of unrequited love that leads the mermaid heroine to transform herself into what she is not.

READING PLAN

This is another tale that can be read and explored on many different levels and with very different age groups. In the following themes you will find some serious issues for high-school students and adults to tackle and others that are readily accessible to all of us. This is a longer story, so it might be worth taking your time with it and breaking it up into sections.

The words paint beautiful pictures, so including some art projects might be a welcome opportunity. Do not rush to the Disney version, tempting though that might be!

THEMES TO EXPLORE

Adventure

The little mermaid is an adventurous heroine. While we might see her as a tragic figure, she has ventured out beyond her sea home and followed her dreams to see the world, even with the challenges clearly before her. "Let's go on an adventure!" can solicit positive responses from children. Their natural curiosity about the world leads them to want to see, hear, feel, and experience everything. What makes an adventure, well, adventurous? Why does the invitation to an adventure excite us but perhaps also make us a bit apprehensive?

Activity

What would you need to have to go on an adventure to . . .

Adventure to . . .	I would bring . . .	I would see . . .	I would do . . .	This is not an adventure because . . .
The zoo				
Disney World				
Your local beach or park				
Your grandparents' house				
The playground				
A lake for fishing				
The Grand Canyon				
Your backyard				

Discussion Questions

1. What kind of adventure would you like to go on? Write down two examples and share with others.
2. What makes some activity into an adventure? List what you think are the key ingredients.
3. Can you have an adventure visiting a place you are very familiar with?
4. Can you have an adventure by yourself or only with others? Why?
5. Do you need to be courageous to go on an adventure?
6. What makes an adventure a good one? A bad one?

Activity: Describing the Important Qualities of an Adventure

Circle the words that you think best capture what makes an adventure an adventure:

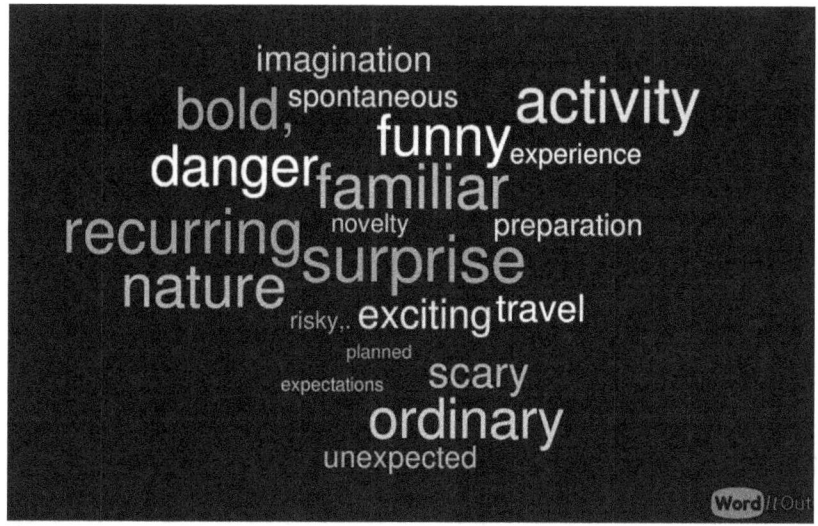

Figure 10.2

Why did you choose each word and which ones did you leave out?

Wishing

The little mermaid has many desires that provoke her to make the choices she does. She wishes to rise to the top and see the above-sea world, she wishes to know the prince, she wishes to become human, and despite her own deep desires, she wishes the prince to be happy with his new bride. There is an old saying, "If wishes were horses, beggars would ride." How might you interpret that?

Wishing is a cognitive state accompanied by feelings of varying strengths. It references a counterfactual, something that is not true but that we would like to be true. It can look to the past, present, or future. Wishing can become a strong catalyst to action through choices.

Many fairy tales include wishing as a key ingredient to drive forward the narrative. We will encounter wishes in other fairy tale chapters. In some cases wishes are made to come true through magic and while this is somewhat the case in the story here, we also find a strong presence of personal agency on the part of the little mermaid.

Discussion Questions

1. How many wishes did the little mermaid make in this story? See if you can find them all.
2. What is the difference between a wish and an idea?
3. What is the difference between a wish and a feeling?
4. Are all wishes good? Why yes or why no?
5. How can a wish come true? What needs to happen? Offer an example to help you explain your response.
6. What does the expression, "Be careful what you wish for" mean?

Activity

Go around the circle and ask each child/young person to share a wish. Alternatively, they could write them down and put them in a pot with or without their names. (You might want to lay out some ground rules: no wish should be hurtful to another person or mean-spirited.) After the wishes have been shared, have a community of inquiry, which addresses the following aspects of wishing:

A wish that is easy to fulfill	A wish about the present
A wish that is hard to fulfill	A wish about the future
An impossible wish	A wish for self
A wish about the past	A wish for others

Have the group add other criteria that seem appropriate based on the choices.

Being Different

One of the more tragic themes in this story is the difference between mermaids and humans. In particular, Andersen depicts mermaids as nonhumans or perhaps as nonpersons in the sense that they lack immortal souls and when they die they simply vanish. Humans after death are transformed and live on in some way. While this is not explicitly stated, clearly the little mermaid feels she is second-best or lacking because of this difference. So she longs to be a human and that is symbolized physically with having two legs and living on land. She accepts deep suffering and agony so as to be or seem to be a human being. But to be human she must give up essential parts of her being: not only her mermaid tail but also her voice.

The theme of losing one's voice is offered later. Here we find a disturbing cautionary tale of trying to be what one is not and ultimately not succeeding.

A dark theme indeed but one that children and young people—and adults—face daily. Being me does not mean that I cannot change at all but there may be limits to the change that are helpful, right, good, and even possible. Teens may be particularly sensitive to this theme as they struggle to both find themselves but also fit into the world around them.

Discussion Questions

1. How is the little mermaid different from human beings?
2. Why does she long to be a human being? What do humans have or can do that she cannot?
3. What might be the advantages and disadvantages for her to change into a human?
4. What does it mean to be yourself?
5. Can you be yourself and still change?
6. In some sense, everyone is different from others so when do the differences matter? Examples may help illustrate your responses here.
7. Why might we long both to be different and to be like others?

Activity

In the following chart fill in the empty boxes and discuss your responses with others to think about differences. See if you can offer your own examples of being different.

Characteristic that could be different for different people	Where it might matter	Where it does not matter	Is change possible? Why or why not?
Your height			
Your ability to sing			
Eyesight			
Shouting out in class			
Being shy			
Playing a sport			
Learning math			
Being a farmer			
Reading			
Being Italian			
Speaking English			
Eating meat			

The Power of Having a Voice

The little mermaid must suffer having her tongue cut out to gain her legs. This renders her unable to speak or to sing in her beautiful voice. While she can try to communicate with her eyes and her dancing, this definitely interferes with her relating to the prince. While she struggles to express her feelings, he clearly does not get what she wants to convey.

However, not being heard or not having a voice is a powerful theme in discussions about race and gender. For centuries women have been ignored or actually silenced so as to keep them in "their place." This continues today but it can also apply to people of color and immigrants whose lack of knowledge of the native language handicaps them in that society. They cannot "speak." We might add children to this group as well. "Children should be seen but not heard" is an old saying. Children have been voiceless in that we do not really listen to them nor take what they say seriously. After all, "they are only children."

In many contexts a child must have an adult literally speak for them for their wants and needs to be attended. In this story our heroine chooses to give up her voice so that she can have the right body so as to pursue her prince. This could be seen from a feminist perspective as a disturbing message indeed. Are girls and women asked to change themselves to be worthy of men? Teens and adults might want to explore this theme in its darker implications.

Discussion Questions

1. Why does the little mermaid give up her voice?
2. What humans and other creatures cannot speak?
3. If you cannot speak, how does that affect your experiences in the world?
4. In past eras, and in some places yet today, women are considered to be "voiceless"—not literally but politically—where or when has this happened? See if you can find some examples to share and discuss.
5. Children are often able to speak but are not listened to or their words are not counted. What does this tell us about children? About adults?
6. Are there others who are capable of speaking but seem to be "voiceless"? Offer examples and explore what these examples reveal.

Activity

Teens and adults may wish to explore the laws that prevented women from making their own decisions and "having a voice," in everything from owning property, attending school, leaving a marriage to voting as citizens. Early proponents of allowing women to control their own lives are John Stuart

Mill and the early feminists, such as Mary Wollstonecraft—both British and important advocates for human rights in the eighteenth and nineteenth centuries. In the United States we find the early feminists in the nineteenth century advocating for voting rights for women. More recently there has been advocacy for children's rights (see the UN Declaration of the Rights of the Child, dating from 1959).

This project would be a great essay or poster project. To connect it to fairy tales, invite them to explore other fairy tales where women cannot speak or are acted upon while they are asleep (another form of passivity).

Rejection

Ultimately the little mermaid is rejected by her prince, without his even realizing he is doing this. He never understands her deep romantic desires for him and treats her like a cherished pet. But the rejection is deeply felt by her and she suffers for the absence of his love. While this makes her plight all that sadder, we do recognize that rejection is part of life. Rarely do we get all we wish for or want from others and from the world.

Learning to deal with rejection makes us resilient and perhaps this is symbolized in the story by her transformation into a creature of the air with the potential to gain that immortal soul and all it promises. Perhaps for Andersen this was the far better outcome than marriage to the prince. But for most modern readers, they will be disappointed that she does not get her prince in the end as would happen in most fairy tales.

Discussion Questions

1. In this fairy tale, the little mermaid is ultimately unsuccessful in getting the prince to marry her. Did he reject her? Why or why not?
2. Even if you decided he did not reject her, was she rejected?
3. Was the prince a bad person for his behavior? Explain your response.
4. How would you describe the relationship between something/someone rejecting and something/someone being rejected?
5. Is being rejected always a bad thing? Why yes or no? Offer some examples.
6. If we feel rejected, how might we deal with our feelings? List possible activities or sources of action that might help.
7. In what sense can a rejection offer us a positive learning experience?
8. Many famous writers and inventors encountered rejections time after time. But in the end, they claim these experiences made them stronger and they persevered. Explore what "resilience" means.

Activity

Comment on the following examples of rejection and discuss with your group. Each team should add a scenario for the entire group to discuss.

Scenario of rejection	Course of action to take	Fair or unfair? Add to the story to clarify	Could this be a good experience?
James was not admitted to his first choice college			
Rob's girlfriend leaves him for his best friend, Tim			
Maggie did not make the travel soccer team			
Sara is always last because her last name begins with a "Z"			
Rachel asks to go to a concert past her curfew and her parents say no			

Happily Ever after?

Does this fairy tale end happily or sadly? Is the story a tragedy or a true fairy tale? Have your child, young person, or group share what they think of the ending. If the prince had married her, would that be a better ending? If she had killed the prince and regained her mermaid self, would that be a happy ending?

Activity

Share these ideas with your young person and see what they think.

Chapter 11

The Seven Ravens

Figure 11.1
Credit Line: Alice V. Gerhardstein

Chapter 11

PLOT

While animal transformations are fairly common in fairy tales, this particular tale is not particularly well known. A man has seven sons but truly wanted a daughter. When his wife indicates she is pregnant, he hopes for that girl and yes, when the baby is born it is a little girl. Since the baby does not seem to be very healthy, they want to baptize her right away and he sends one of his sons to the well to get water. The other six scamper off after him and at the well they end up competing to see who can get the water first and the bucket falls deep in the well. Stunned, they do not know what to do.

The father is waiting impatiently and when they do not return immediately he senses that they were playing and angrily curses them by wishing they would all turn into ravens. Poof! He hears the flutter of bird wings and as he looks up, he spies seven ravens flying off in the distance. There is nothing he can say or do to take back the spell. Be careful what you wish for.

Luckily the daughter survives and grows up to be beautiful and kind. Her parents never mention the sons as they do not want her to feel bad but other people whisper that she is the reason the sons have met such a terrible fate. When she confronts her parents, they reassure her that while the seven brothers had been transformed into ravens, it was not her fault. However, she feels that she indeed was the cause for this misfortune, and she determines to find them. Packing only a small ring to remind her of her parents, a loaf of bread, and some water, off she goes into the wide world.

She first encounters the sun but it was too hot and, as she believes, eats little children. Next she meets the moon but the moon is too cold and also scary. When she comes across the stars, they are more friendly and kind. The morning star offers her a small wishbone, which she claims will help her open up the glass mountain. Off our heroine goes after wrapping the little bone carefully in a cloth.

However, when she arrives at the glass mountain, she finds the gate locked. She opens up her cloth only to discover the bone has slipped out. What to do? She takes a knife and cuts off her small finger, which serves as a key and unlocks the door. There she finds a dwarf who confirms that the seven ravens are not at home but will be returning soon. He sets the table with plates of food and cups of wine. Hungry, the little girl take a bite from each plate and a sip from each cup. In the last cup, she puts the ring.

When the ravens fly in, they begin to eat but notice that someone has taken a bite and a sip from each plate and cup. Who has been eating from my plate? Who has been drinking from my cup? The last one finds the ring and recognizes it. If their sister is there they will be saved, he exclaims. She pops out from behind a door and the ravens are transformed back into boys. They hug and kiss and make their way back home.

READING PLAN

This tale may be a new one for your audience, although there are a number of fairy tales where boys are transformed into swans or other kinds of birds and must have their sister rescue them through sacrifice. Magic, animal transformation, and love feature in this imaginative tale. This story will appeal to young children and older ones alike.

Read this story out loud or share the reading in a circle. Do not hesitate to stop during the story to see if there are opportunities for discussion or exploring a theme. Remember that the themes can take us far away from the story itself and in a philosophy discussion that is perfectly fine. Do not be surprised if your audience finds other ideas emerge in the story and try to follow their lead in setting the inquiry.

THEMES

Misbehaving

In the beginning of this story, the father is upset because he has given one of his sons an important task and as all seven of them ran off together, he is pretty sure they are playing around and not doing what he asked. What really happened is that they were competing to see who could get to the well first and with pushing and shoving, the bucket fell down the well. I guess we could say they were misbehaving.

Children are well aware of the rules of behavior and are often chastised when they break them by misbehaving. Who makes the rules for behavior? How do we learn what they are? Which ones may be cultural and which ones might be more broadly ethical rules?

Discussion Questions

1. Did the boys misbehave when they were trying to get the water? Or were they all trying to help?
2. Can someone misbehave without meaning to do so?
3. Do you misbehave if no one knows you did so? Explain your response.
4. From where do the rules of behavior come?
5. Can there be different sets of rules for behavior? Illustrate your response with examples.
6. Why are the rules of behavior important? Or are they?
7. Are some misbehaviors worse than others? Give examples and reasons for why you said yes or no.

8. Are the rules of behavior the same as good manners?
9. Are good manners the same as being a good person? Why yes or no?

Wishes

In this tale the father inadvertently turns his sons into ravens when they fail to return promptly from their task. Wishing for something captures a cognitive and an affective dimension. We think of something that is not or that we do not have and we intend toward a state where we indeed would have it. Wishes can be a simple as a birthday wish when blowing out candles or as complex as wishing one's grandmother would get well. Wishes can consume us to the point that we are obsessed with desire or they can motivate us to make real changes that lead to wish fulfillment.

In this tale the frustrated and worried father wishes his sons would become ravens and fly off. Unfortunately his wish is granted, even if he immediately regrets it. Magic is not a real force in our lives but the unfortunate consequences to wishing can be very real.

Discussion Questions

1. The father wished his sons to be turned into ravens. Do you think he really meant this to happen? What in the story supports your position?
2. How would you describe the nature of a wish?
3. How many kinds of wishes can you think of? Some examples might include a birthday wish, wishing on a star—what would you add?
4. Can you wish about something that has already happened?
5. Are wishes good or bad? How could we differentiate between them?
6. Giving an example, show how to make a wish come true.

Activity

Fill in the following chart and discuss your examples and reasons with others in your group.

Examples of a wish	Would an adult, child, or teen wish for this?	Good wish? Why	Bad wish? why	Could this come true?— and why yes or no
I wish for a new car				
I wish to be picked for the travel soccer team				

Examples of a wish	Would an adult, child, or teen wish for this?	Good wish? Why	Bad wish? why	Could this come true?— and why yes or no
I wish that my teacher would get sick and cancel school				
I wish for a millions dollars				
I wish I had a dark tan				
I wish I could grow five inches taller				
I wish my son gets into college				
I wish I were dead				
I wish I had a puppy				
I wish mom was not so mean and would let me stay out late				

Responsibility

The young girl felt responsible for the plight of her brothers. It was because she was such a sickly baby that her parents wanted to get her baptized so quickly and sent the sons off to fetch water. But she herself did not ask them to do this. But can a baby be responsible at all? When do we become responsible for our actions? If you feel responsible, does that mean you are so?

These are important questions to explore with children and young people. But adults as well struggle to determine the extent of personal responsibility.

Discussion Questions

1. When the young girl finds out about her missing brothers, she feels very responsible for their transformation into ravens. The father who issued the wish also feels bad that he has lost his sons. Which of these characters do you find the more responsible for this action, if either?
2. Can you be responsible for actions you did not intend or mean to happen?
3. Can you be responsible if you wished something to happen but did not act on it? That is, can we be responsible for our thoughts and feelings which come out as wishes?

4. Can babies be responsible for anything? What if yes, and why? If you answered no, why not?
5. When should we hold someone to be responsible for some action or deed?
6. Are there actions of events for which no one is responsible?
7. Which is more important to establish responsibility: that a person caused an action to happen or that they intended it to happen? Or are both equally important?

Activity

Use the following chart to start a discussion about responsibility. Note: some of these examples may be best suited for young adults or adults. You can substitute other scenarios if you are uncomfortable with the example for your group.

Action	Who/what might be responsible if anyone/anything	Should they be praised, blamed, or are they not responsible at all?	Your reasons
Picking the joker when playing cards			
A hurricane floods out Aaron's family home which is built right near the shoreline			
The teacher failed Joey in math			
Jenn makes fun of her ex-friend in popular social media accounts			
The summer camp chooses not to hire Fred because of what he posts on social media about hating kids and animals			
Joan loses her gloves . . . for the third time this winter			
Maggie gets the measles because her parents did not get her vaccinated			

Action	Who/what might be responsible if anyone/anything	Should they be praised, blamed, or are they not responsible at all?	Your reasons
Timmy's dog ran away because he was rushing to get into the house and did not close the door fully			
Timmy's mom left the back gate open, hoping the dog would get out and stop barking at the back door			
Rover, Timmy's dog, ran out into the street when he found the chance to do it			
James picked up all the sports equipment after the game to help out his coach			
Sarai got first chair in the school orchestra			

Ravens and Birds

Ravens are beautiful black birds, rather larger than crows. Birds have always fascinated human beings with their ability to fly high in the sky. Ancient people saw them as messengers from the gods or simply as messengers in general. The Romans would study the entrails of birds as a fortune-telling exercise. One might wonder from where they got this idea.

While this might not be properly a philosophical topic, it can be interesting to learn more about animals to better appreciate their world. We have explored birds in other fairy tales but since they are so prominent in this one, you might wish to develop a project around birds.

Project: Learning about Birds

The boys are transformed into ravens when their father utters that fateful wish. Would you like to be a bird? Why or why not? What do you know about birds, for example—about ravens? What is the difference between crows, blackbirds, and ravens? See if you can find some information about these kinds of birds and make a picture book or poster to help others understand these kinds of birds. Consider these kinds of questions and topics:

- Where do these birds live?
- What do they eat and what kind of nests do they build?
- How might one recognize their eggs and their young?
- How have humans related to these different kinds of birds?
- Are any of these birds endangered?
- Do we know anything about how smart these birds are?
- Do any of these birds make good pets? Why or why not?
- Are birds a form of pest? Or do they offer valuable services to humans and other animals?
- Should we care about birds?

Journey

In this tale the young girl—we do not know her age—takes a perilous journey in the hopes of rescuing her brothers. Without a plan and with the bare necessities, she sets out alone to find them. While we do not encourage our children to go off on their own—far from it!—we can enter into the magic of this tale and admire her for her plucky courage. It may be significant that this is a young girl venturing forth, rather than a young man or boy. Girls can have adventures too! In some way, every one of us takes a journey through our life.

Discussion Questions

1. Why does the girl leave home on her journey and what is significant about what she takes with her?
2. Can someone go on a journey without knowing where they are going?
3. Is a journey the same as an adventure, a trip, or a bit different? Explain your response.
4. How long does a journey need to be to be a real journey?
5. Are all journeys physical ones through space?
6. Some people say that "life is a journey." Do you agree?
7. Have you ever taken a journey? Write a short paragraph or essay about your journey.

Sacrifice

Our heroine braves the scary sun and moon, both of which apparently eat children, and ends up cutting off her own little finger to make a key to get into the Glass Mountain. She is willing to suffer and to give up part of her own body to save her brothers. This is a startling turn in the story but perhaps significant of the depth of her desire to save them—perhaps based on the belief of her own culpability in their original enchantment.

Many a fairy tale recounts a significant sacrifice that must be made to help another. But we also saw sacrifices to help one's self, consider the two stepsisters in *Cinderella* as examples. So, perhaps all sacrifices are not to be admired?

Discussion Questions

1. What does the young girl sacrifice to help save her brothers? What does this tell us about her character?
2. The boys lost their human form when they transformed into ravens. Did they sacrifice anything? Why or why not?
3. Does sacrifice require bravery? How yes or why not?
4. Could a sacrifice ever be a bad thing to do? Explain.
5. What sacrifices have you seen people make? You can choose someone you know or someone from history or the news.

Chapter 12
Cinderella

Figure 12.1
Credit Line: Alice V. Gerhardstein

Chapter 12

PLOT

Perhaps no fairy tale is as well known as Cinderella. But you can find many different versions of this story. The Charles Perrault version, the inspiration for the Disney movie, introduces the fairy godmother and at the end Cinderella compassionately invites her mean sisters to live with her and finds them rich husbands.

Not so much in the Grimm version, however. The Grimm brothers begin their version with the same loss of a beloved mother who promises her little daughter that if she is good, the mother will look down from heaven and watch over her. The reference to heaven was most likely introduced by the Grimm brothers to include a Christian theme within the story. The new wife comes with two stepdaughters who are described as quite beautiful but not very nice. They take away from Cinderella her dresses and toys and banish her to the kitchen to be a servant.

As in many fairy tales, her father does nothing to intervene. When he goes off to a fair, the two stepdaughters ask for beautiful things but Cinderella asks for a branch that brushes by him. So he brings her home a shoot from a hazel tree, which she plants on her mother's grave. A gala is announced by the king at which the prince will choose his bride. The two sisters are all agog and when Cinderella asks to go they give her a series of impossible tasks as a deterrent.

As you can suspect, animals are her friends due to her innate kindness and the birds of the air come and help her sort the lentils from the ashes. She does this twice but despite being successful, the mother and sisters leave her at home. She goes to the hazel tree and asks it to shower "gold and silver down on me" and the tree obligingly does so. She has a beautiful dress with golden slippers and off she goes to the ball.

Of course, when she arrives everyone is astounded by her beauty and the prince dances with no one else all evening. At evening's end she escapes and hurries back home to return her dress to the tree and put on her sooty smock. This happens two more times. Each time her dress is more elaborate and stunning. On the third night the price puts pitch on the stairs which captures one of her dainty shoes. In the Grimm version, the father is at the dance and muses each time, "could this be Cinderella?"

On the following morning the prince visits all young women in the kingdom to find the owner of the shoe. Each of the stepsisters tries on the shoe but for one, her toe is too big. The mother counsels her to cut it off which she does. As the prince is ready to ride away with his false bride, the birds call out the deception, telling him to look at the blood in the shoe. The second sister slices off a piece of her heel and the birds likewise sound the alarm.

He asks if any girls remain and the father mentions his first daughter but dismisses her as puny. When she appears she has washed her face and hands and the prince recognizes her, despite the shabby clothes. As they ride off, the birds acclaim that this time he got it right. The tale ends with the wedding but again the birds get the last word as they peck out the eyes of the two jealous stepsisters as they enter and leave the church.

There are some interesting patterns in the Grimm's version. Note that events happen in threes in this tale. This is a common pattern in fairy tales. There are three sisters, three opportunities for Cinderella to earn a place at the ball, three days for the prince to dance and choose his bride. Birds feature prominently as helpers and messengers from her deceased mother. Cinderella is close to the natural world, which rallies to help her against the cruelty of humans. Kindness triumphs and evil is punished.

TARGETED AGE LEVEL

As one of the most popular and familiar fairy tales, many young children will delight in this story. You can find many different versions, some less gruesome as that offered by the Grimm's and the pattern can be found cross-culturally as well. It has inspired countless movies and other stories, which keep the format of beleaguered but good young woman who is saved by her prince in some form or fashion.

In choosing your story version, pick one which offers some opportunities to explore the nuances of this tale. You can tailor this exploration to your audience, be it kindergartners or high-school kids, by choosing a particular version of the tale or by following their interest in such themes as offered later.

READING PLAN

As always, read the story afresh and encourage your child or group to make note of interesting or troubling words, events, or ideas that occur to them. When doing philosophy, it is not so important that we stay within the story. We can follow the ideas where they take us, even if in the end it has nothing to do with the story before us.

The Grimm's version has explicit violence that may be of morbid fascination to children, especially since it is connected to punishing the evil sisters. Teens may wish to question the courtship ritual that sounds both bizarre and possibly demeaning to women. They may wish to discuss our view of birds and what they contribute to our life in an ecological sense. Be willing to follow the comments and questions where they go, and do not be overly concerned about sticking to the story.

THEMES TO EXPLORE

Jealousy

We all experience jealousy and siblings are certainly prone to thinking their brother or sister is favored. In *Cinderella*, we find the two sisters acting in ways that could signal they are jealous of Cinderella and are anxious to demote her in the eyes of her father. Jealousy is a complex emotion that evokes negative comparisons between one's self and someone else. Can jealousy be a positive force for us to improve or does it simply allow me to feel better by denigrating the other person?

Discussion Questions

1. Are the two sisters jealous of Cinderella? Why yes or no?
2. Can we be jealous of the following?
    a. Our cat
    b. Our sister or brother
    c. Our teacher
    d. Our best friend
    e. The president
    f. Strangers we see on a train
    g. Our parents
3. Can you feel jealous but not act on it?
4. Can you act jealous but not feel it?
5. Can you be jealous of someone if you do not know them?
6. What seems worse to you, feeling jealous or acting jealously? Why?
7. Is jealousy a bad feeling to have? If yes, why?

Activity

What are the shared characteristics that seem to lead to one feeling jealousy? Use the word bank below to help you construct an explanation of jealousy:

Figure 12.2

Birds

Birds feature prominently in this story. They support Cinderella and come to her rescue a number of times to sort the lentils and then inform the prince that he was taking the wrong bride twice. At the end they punish the two sisters by brutally pecking out their eyes. Birds seem to inhabit a middle world between the ground upon which we live and the sky where metaphorically the angels live.

In our world birds not only are harbingers of spring but also can warn us of the dangers of climate change. Way back in 1962, biologist Rachel Carson published *Silent Spring* that highlighted the dangers of pesticides and how their use was killing birds and other animal species.

Discussion Questions

1. In *Cinderella*, Cinderella often calls on birds to help her and they do. What kinds of birds come to her aid?
2. How many times can you find a bird or birds helping her?
3. Doves feature in this tale. What do doves often symbolize in stories?
4. What fascinates us about birds? Would you like to be a bird? If yes, why and if no, why not?
5. Can birds communicate? How so, if yes?
6. When a parrot or parakeet talks in a human language, does it know what it is saying?
7. Birds are living creatures. Should we treat them as morally significant? Why or why not?
8. Did the birds do the right thing in the end of the story? Discuss what you think of their actions.

Activities

1. Choose a bird that is local to your area and investigate everything you can about your bird. Create a poster to share with your group about your bird: its markings, behaviors, nest formation, and relationship to other birds. Is your bird local to your environment or was it introduced from a different ecosystem?
2. Create a list of intelligence in birds and compare birds with mammals and humans. For some resources, consider the following articles available online:

    "Why Ravens and Crows Are Earth's Smartest Birds" by Amelia Stymacks, https://news.nationalgeographic.com/2018/03/year-of-the-bird-brains-intelligence-smarts/

    An article from the Audobon Society, "Bird IQ Tests: 8 Ways Researchers Test Bird Intelligence," https://www.audubon.org/news/bird-iq-tests-8-ways-researchers-test-bird-intelligence

    If birds are intelligent, should we treat them differently than we currently do?

Patterns of Three

As mentioned earlier, many things in this tale occur in three. This is not uncommon in fairy tales where there can be three siblings, three doors, three wishes, and so on. We might see this as a device to signal alternatives, chances, or contrasts. It might be intriguing for your child or children to encourage them to note these repetitive patterns and investigate how many times this tale uses three as a device. If you are working with a group, pair them up and have them go through the story to work on the following challenge.

Activity

In *Cinderella*, we often find patterns of three. See how many examples you can find in the story where the number three occurs. Why do you think these patterns are used in the story? Hint: there are at least seven examples.

Choosing Friends/Partners

In our fairy tale, princes pick wives on the basis of three days of balls. This may seem like a rather questionable process for choosing a life partner. Although for most of history, the aristocrats or wealthy saw marriage more as a financial and political arrangement rather than any kind of love match. We also learn very little about the nature of the prince. So, what do we know about him? If your children are interested, it might be worth exploring both the criteria he uses to choose his princess as well as think more broadly about friendship.

Discussion Questions

1. What did the prince use to choose his princess? How many criteria can you determine from his actions? (Possible responses: her beauty, her clothes, her dancing ability, her small feet, her novelty, . . .)
2. The prince plays a trick on Cinderella by pouring sticky pitch on the stairway. Was this an action that was good to do? Why or why not?
3. Should our friends be like us or different from us? Why?
4. Do boys choose friends in a different way than girls do? Why yes or no? If yes, how so?
5. Can an animal be a good friend? Why yes or why no?
6. What do you think is the most important characteristic in a friend?
7. Is a bad friend still a friend?
8. If you change, must you change your friends?

Activity: Choosing Friends

What criteria do you think are best to use when choosing a friend or a partner? Add some at the end and discuss your responses with your group.

Characteristic	Good criteria	Bad or irrelevant criteria	Why?
Beautiful or good-looking			
Speaks the same language			
Likes what you like			
Is adventurous and fun			
Your family likes them			
Shares your culture			
Introduces you to new ideas and activities			
Is a lot older or younger than you			

Loyalty

Loyalty is a key virtue. Despite ethical theories that demand we treat all people equally, in fact we do not. We do owe more to our families, friends, and acquaintances over strangers. This does not mean we have no obligation toward others but our level of obligation moves out in concentric circles. In *Cinderella*, we find Cinderella is loyal to her mother and her mother's memory. She plants a tree, cares for it, and visits it. But we do not get any sense that her stepsisters show any loyalty to her nor she to them. Her stepmother clearly lacks any sense of loyalty to Cinderella.

Discussion Questions

1. Who would you say is a loyal person in this story?
2. Do we earn loyalty or is loyalty an automatic obligation in some cases? Which ones, if the latter?
3. If someone is loyal to you, must you be loyal back to them? Explain your response.
4. Can you be too loyal to someone? When, if yes?
5. Why do we value loyalty as an important virtue in so many settings: family, among friends, in the military?

Sisters

Many fairy tales include siblings; some are competitive, while others are supportive. In *Cinderella*, the stepsisters are depicted as jealous and mean-spirited. Most tales, which include blended families, seem to address competition and jealousy as part of being not a "real" mother, brother, or sister. Interestingly enough, in the older versions of this tale the sisters are described as quite beautiful, which is not the case with the classic movie version.

In many fairy tales one's outward appearance directly reflects one's inner character: physically beautiful people are nice and kind, while ugly people are mean or cruel. In spite of their beauty, these stepsisters do all they can to humiliate their sister. What are the elements of sisterhood or sibling relationships? Must we like our brothers or sisters? Are they like us or can they be quite different, even if they share the same parents? And why do fairy tales so often present sisters and brothers in an adversarial role?

Discussion Questions

1. In *Cinderella*, the stepsisters are described as quite beautiful but not very nice. What makes them beautiful? What makes them not very nice?
2. Fairy tales often introduce stepsisters as mean or unfair. Why do you think they do this?
3. If you are a stepsister or stepbrother, what does that mean?
4. Do we always love our sisters/brothers? How so or why not?

5. Do we always love our stepsisters/stepbrothers? How so or why not? Did you answer this question differently than #3? Discuss.
6. Do you have to be friends with your sister? Explain.
7. Should all children in one family be treated alike? Discuss your answer.
8. Can you love your sister but not like her?
9. Should we be loyal to our sister or brother? And should that be different if they are our stepsister or brother?
10. Do we owe our sisters or brothers more care and concern than we owe friends? Than we owe strangers? Explain your answer.

Activity

If you have a brother or sister, come up with five words that you think describe your relationship with him or her. List on index cards, one per card. Spread them all on a table to share with others to see how many match, how many are similar, and how many are very different, maybe even contradictory.

Sacrifice

The story of Cinderella introduces us to the idea of sacrifice—what we are willing to give up or do and why. Sacrifices can be seen as extraordinary acts of helping someone else but they may also generate resentment and be done for all the wrong reasons. In this tale we find Cinderella trying her best to do what will endear her to her family, to help them accept her, but nothing suffices. What has she sacrificed to be a member of the family? And the sisters each maim their feet at the insistence of their mother so as to fit into the slipper offered by the prince.

The pain and suffering are vividly described by the chanting birds who point out the blood oozing out of their shoes. In the end their selfishness and deceit leads to them losing their eyesight as the birds punish them. This is tough stuff! Sacrifice is one of those virtues that must be calibrated to the situation and purpose to determine its moral value. But in many cases it does indeed represent the highest ethical aspiration.

Discussion Questions

1. Does Cinderella have to give up anything in this story? Do we admire her for her actions or do we think she might be making bad decisions? Why?
2. What do the sisters sacrifice? Was this a sign of their generosity? Why yes or why no?

3. What does it mean to "sacrifice" something or one's self? What makes a sacrifice an action we admire or praise versus an action we question or judge?
4. Is making a sacrifice always a good deed? Why yes or why no?

Activity

Think about the nature of sacrifice in terms of the following aspects. An "agent" is the person who is acting to do something. A "patient" is the recipient of some action. For example, if a boy gives up his lunch to help a fellow student, he is the agent and the fellow student is the patient or recipient. The components would be: what he sacrificed (his lunch), how he did it (publicly, privately? with grace or grudgingly), the motive is why he gave up his lunch or why the child accepted/rejected it and the effect is how that sacrifice affected both him and the receiving child.

To put it another way:

What was sacrificed?
Why was it sacrificed?
How was it sacrificed?
Who was the actor/agent and who was the recipient/patient?

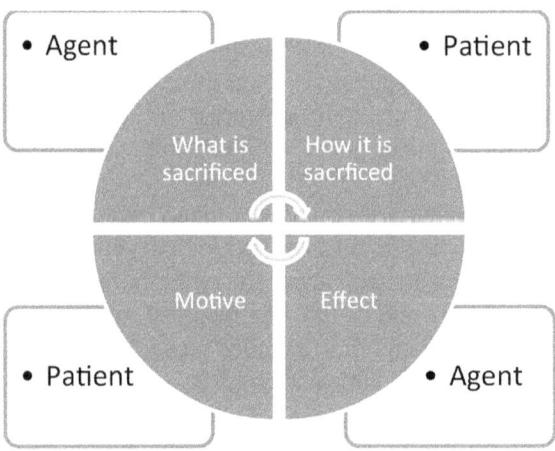

Figure 12.3

Chapter 13

Beauty and the Beast

Figure 13.1
Credit Line: Alice V. Gerhardstein

PLOT

This fairy tale has many ancient forms but is most familiar in its literary presentation by the French woman Jeanne-Marie Leprince de Beaumont, an eighteenth-century aristocratic writer. The story begins with a wealthy merchant who has six children, three boys and three girls, the youngest of which is so beautiful that she has acquired the nickname of "Beauty." As you can guess, her sisters do not appreciate how she is lauded over them but Beauty has a kind and gentle nature to match her physical beauty while the sisters are mean-spirited and envious.

When the merchant's fortunes are lost at sea, they have to move to the country and while the boys help out and Beauty runs the house, the two sisters mope around and complain. When the father receives notice that one of his ships may have survived, they are all overjoyed at the prospect of regaining their wealth and status and each girl asks for fancy gifts from town. But Beauty simply asks for a rose.

As it turns out, the ship did not arrive as expected and on his way home, the merchant became lost in the snowy woods, ending up in a magical castle. No one seems to be there but he receives food and a warm bed for the night. In the morning he is about to leave when he sees a lovely rose and breaks it off. A terrible beast appears and insists that, since the merchant stole from him, he must return with a daughter for the beast or take the place himself.

Beauty's love her for father leads her to insist that she go back with him, over her father's reluctance and the barely suppressed delight of the sisters who look forward to her demise at the hands of the beast. Beauty accompanies her father to the palace and is left there. Over the next weeks she meets the beast each evening and while initially scared of him, she gradually begins to enjoy his companionship. Every evening, however, she refuses his offer of marriage, although as politely as she can.

Upon requesting the opportunity to visit her father who she can see in a magic mirror is mourning her assumed demise, Beauty is granted a visit by the beast but he warns her that if she does not return in a week, he will die. She promises to do so.

Her visit home is a joyful one although the sisters who have meanwhile married rather unpleasant men are jealous of all her finery. They decide to ruin her by pretending to miss her and beg her to stay longer. Beauty agrees to do so as they seem so genuine. They assume that her breaking the promise to return in a week will so enrage the beast that he will eat her for sure.

When Beauty has a vision that the beast is dying, she quickly takes her ring off, as instructed, putting it on her night table, and when she awakes, she is back in the palace.

That evening she awaits her friend but he does not show up; she rushes out to the garden and finds him virtually dead. She promises to marry him and claims that she has loved him after all.

Poof! In the place of the beast is a handsome prince who had been transformed into the beast because he was so ungrateful and spoiled. Only if a beauty was willing to marry him as a beast could he be saved. The palace comes alive, her family appears, but the two sisters are turned into stone statues. They can only be transformed back again if they repent and the fairy who wields this power indicates she is doubtful that either of them will ever change.

Unlike the popular Disney retelling, there is no crude suitor trying to marry Beauty nor do the townspeople pick up weapons to kill him. Justice is meted out at the end to the two mean sisters and Beauty and her transformed Beast live happily ever after . . . we assume.

TARGETED AGE LEVEL

This tale is recognized and well loved by all ages. However, you will find much here to generate some excellent conversation among teens and older children. They are acutely aware of how important beauty is in their circles and the following themes, which suggest this might merit some careful analysis, should interest them.

READING PLAN

This version is a delightful story to read and one of the longer fairy tales. The readers will find quite a bit of lecturing within the de Beaumont's version as clearly this was a tale to be told as a moral lesson. At the same time, its familiarity and imagery will capture children and young people. A number of fairy tales present potential grooms as animals. Some have suggested that this captures the unknown nature of the male for the young girl who, in earlier times, was married off to a virtual stranger.

When reading this tale with your children and young people, it might be helpful to highlight how this is not the Disney version and to alert the participants to look for points of difference. They will still recognize many similarities, however. Which version do they like better? You might ask them.

THEMES TO EXPLORE

Outcast/Being Left Out

The theme of being an outcast emerges in different parts of the story. Clearly, the beast is an outcast, living by himself in the dark forest. But the merchant and his family are outcast from town society when they lose their money. Beauty is outcast from her family and ultimately she and the beast form a friendship over that status. Children and young people often feel left out by their peers but in some cases even by their families. Adolescents are acutely aware of their status as "in" or "out," which can change within one day in the world of teens. Being an accepted member of one's group is important for all of us and children are no different.

Discussion Questions

1. Which characters in this fairy tale seem to be outcasts or unaccepted by their group?
2. Is it important to be a member of a group? If yes, what kind of group(s) matter?
3. Can someone be included in one group but not in another? If yes, offer an example.
4. Are there certain groups that one should want to be excluded from? If yes, which ones? Why?
5. What defines a group of which one is a member? Give examples to help explain.

Activity

Using a blackboard or whiteboard or a large piece of paper, have the young people each draw a circle to represent a group and label it. Should any of the circles overlap? Some sample groups might be: friends, one's class, family, sports team, musical group (orchestra, band), political party, ethnic or national group. How many groups does a person belong to? Are some groups more important than others? Why or why not?

After drawing the groups, have the young people discuss what criteria or characteristics would make someone an outcast of that group.

Promises III

The theme of making a promise, and keeping it, comes up again and again in fairy tales. The merchant promises his daughters to bring back presents and he must also promise the beast to return by himself or with a daughter. Using these examples (and any other types of promises you find in this tale), explore the question of which promises must be kept and which can be broken, if any—and why.

Discussion Questions

1. Find examples of individuals making promises in this tale. See how many you can find.
2. Are all promises verbal or could you make a promise without saying anything? Explain your response.
3. Why do we so often see keeping promises as an important thing to do?
4. Is there a time limit for keeping a promise?
5. Are there promises we should never make? If yes, which ones? What characterizes them?
6. Are there circumstances when it would be alright to break a promise? Give an example and cite reasons.

Activity

In the following chart decide whether the promise should be made, should be kept, and why.

Promise scenario	Promise should be kept	Promise should not be made	Promise should not be kept	Reasons for your response
Sue promises to help Abel with his homework				
Mike's mother promises him that she will take him to her home country, Colombia, to visit his relatives				
Joan promises to share her exam answers with Alice to help her pass math				
The teacher promises the class that they can play outside after the test				

Promise scenario	Promise should be kept	Promise should not be made	Promise should not be kept	Reasons for your response
Lorelei promises her music teacher that she will not tell anyone about their special relationship				
Joey promises to pay back the five dollars he borrowed from Juan				

Being a Beast

One of the key elements to this fairy tale is the depiction of the scary beast. Illustrators have used their imagination to portray this character in a myriad of ways, each one trying to convey how "beastly" the Beast is. From one perspective this highlights a big distinction between being human and being nonhuman, a beast. Even with language, this beast is still terrifying and Beauty is quite open about how unattractive he looks. At one point she thinks to herself that she could never love anything so ugly. He is too different from humans to be included as a potential husband or partner.

However, over time her feelings change. What initially appeared as "the other," as alien and unacceptable, is transformed into a friend and ultimately into a being she realizes that she deeply loves. This could lead to some intriguing questions about animals and beasts and our relationship to them. But it might also yield some questions and reflections on how what at first appears strange and off-putting can appear quite differently after we get to know that being.

Discussion Questions

1. What do you think the Beast looks like? Draw a picture or find an illustration that captures his beast-like nature best. Share your choice with others and compare. What elements are common? Which ones might be different?
2. Why are both the merchant and Beauty so terrified of the beast?
3. Does labeling a creature as a "beast" reveal some assumptions about beasts? About humans?
4. Often beings that look very different from us are viewed suspiciously and fearfully. Why do you think that is so?

5. Can humans be friends with beasts? Explain your answer and offer some illustrative examples.
6. Are there some beasts that we can never be friends with? Why yes or why no?

Outer/Inner Beauty

Young people have learned quite well to claim that inner beauty is all that matters and external beauty does not. While they may know that this is the "right thing to say," their behaviors often contradict these lofty sentiments. This fairy tale, while ending on a positive note, does offer some opportunities to think carefully about the ideas of inner and outer and to explore how they factor into our real-life experiences. What do we really mean by these terms and should we always accept this platitude, even if there is some truth in it?

Discussion Questions

1. Which characters in this fairy tale are physically beautiful and which have what we call "inner beauty"? And which ones might we say are not beautiful at all?
2. What are the characteristics that make something externally beautiful?
3. Which are the characteristics that make something internally beautiful? Can anything have internal beauty?
4. Can you change your view of what is externally not beautiful? Why or why not?
5. Can you change your view of what is internally beautiful? Again, explain your response.
6. Does the word "beauty" mean the same thing when we are speaking of internal or external?

Activity

Label the following words as referring to internal or external example of beauty, or if you are not sure, use a "?"

Can you add any other examples?

Face	body	actions	thoughts	desires	wishes
Feelings	teeth	eyes	nose	ideas	character
Hair	intentions	speech			

Figure 13.2

Siblings and Jealousy

In this tale the heroine is depicted as good and kind as well as beautiful. Her sisters, not stepsisters, are claimed to be beautiful but not in terms of their actions and behaviors. Her brothers, however, seem to be background characters of little import. Why are the sisters so mean to Beauty? They are glad she might be eaten by the beast and are very jealous when she returns home with beautiful clothes. They pretend to want her to stay and even make themselves cry, but the readers recognize that they are simply being spiteful.

Most of the time we focus on Beauty and the beast, neglecting the motives and actions of the sisters. Perhaps they merit some attention?

Discussion Questions

1. How do Beauty's two sisters behave throughout the story? What might be their reasons?
2. Should Beauty be nice to sisters who treat her so meanly? Why or why not?
3. Is being jealous a natural emotion among siblings? Why or why not?
4. Jealousy is a real emotion and most of us have experienced it as some time or another. What might be some examples of jealousy? Create a scenario to discuss.
5. Could being jealous be a powerful motive to do better? If yes, would that make jealousy a good thing to experience?

Beauty

Of course, Beauty is the name of our heroine in this tale but also descriptive of how she looks and how she acts toward others. Her sisters are also described as beautiful but not in terms of their attitudes, intentions, and behaviors. While Beauty does end up falling in love with the Beast, it is this love which transforms the Beast into a likewise beautiful prince. In the end beauty wins over all but is also elevated to an ultimate value.

How important is it that "The Beast" turns into a handsome young prince? Could Beauty be beautiful without physical beauty? Does this fairy tale reinforce stereotypes of how important looking beautiful is for ultimate success in the world? Teens might wonder if this entire story is not just an affirmation of the importance of looking beautiful as defined by the social world around us.

Discussion Questions

1. The concept of beauty is a central concept in this tale. Where do you find characters and events labeled as beautiful or ugly/not beautiful?
2. How important is beauty in our experiences today?
3. While "beauty" is a well-recognized idea and sought by everyone, what exactly does it mean?
4. We sometimes hear that "beauty is in the eye of the beholder." What does this phrase mean and why might you support it or challenge it? Try to offer reasons for both.
5. If this tale had ended with the Beast and Beauty living happily ever after but as the Beast and as Beauty, would the story be disappointing? Why or why not?

Final Thoughts about *Beauty and the Beast*

In addition to the Disney movie, there are other visual retellings of this story. Find different versions and compare the way the stories are told. What is it that entrances us most about this fairy tale? What might bother us the most?

Chapter 14

Hansel and Gretel

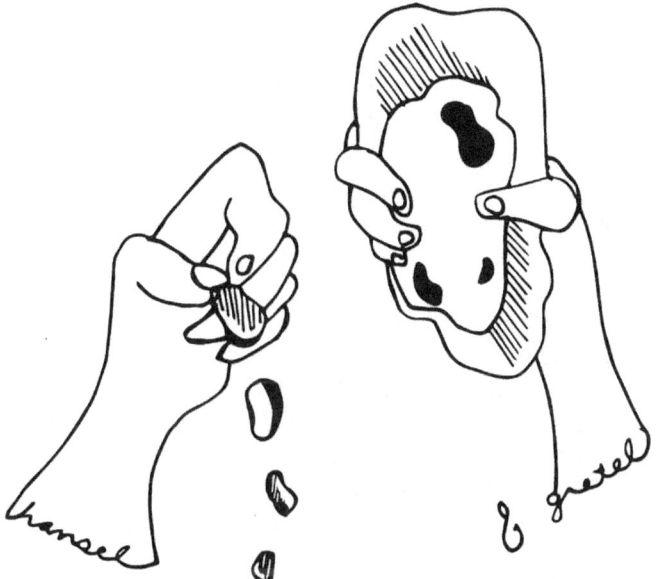

Figure 14.1
Credit Line: Alice V. Gerhardstein

Chapter 14

PLOT

In this well-known tale, we meet a small family during famine time—a mother (or as often recast—a stepmother), a father, and two small children—Hansel and his sister Gretel. Because food is running out, the stepmother suggests taking the children into the forest and abandoning them. Is this to spare the parents watching their children starve or to save more food for the adults? While the father appears to protest, he seems to quickly go along with his wife's plans. But the children overheard this conversation and Hansel has a plan to save them.

After all are asleep, he goes out and fills his pockets with bright white stones. The next day, they depart for the forest and each child is given a piece of bread for their only meal. As they troop along, Hansel lets the white stones slip from him pocket one by one along the path. When they are deep in the forest, the parents build a fire and tell the children to wait while they go to cut wood. The father even sets up a ruse where it sounds as if they are chopping nearby when in fact it is only a piece of wood tied to a branch, making the noise.

After their meager meal, they go to sleep; when they wake up, it is night, but when the moon comes, they follow the glistening white stones back to home. Father is overjoyed to see them but their stepmother not so much.

Several weeks later, the parents plan the abandonment again, but this time Hansel cannot get out at night to pick up stones, so all he has is the small crust of bread given to him in the morning before they set out. He does the same tactic, dropping crumbs along the way. The same sequence of events happens, but this time, when they wake up in the dark from their exhausted sleep, they find no crumbs as the birds have eaten them. They are truly lost.

They wander for a couple of days, following a beautiful bird until they find a lovely little house in the woods. This house is made of bread, cake, and sugar. Who can resist eating a bit? Certainly not the starving children! The door opens and a very old woman pops her head out to see who is eating her home. Note: in the first edition, she is not described as a witch but in many ways her appearance and behavior become emblematic of the witch trope. She invites them in and feeds them a rich repast, after which she tucks them in warm little beds. They go to sleep feeling loved and saved at last!

But in the morning all changes when the witch throws Hansel in a cage and makes Gretel cook, clean, and feed Hansel to fatten him up to eat. Each day she asks Hansel to stick out his finger to see how fat he is becoming but he sticks out a small bone instead. Since she cannot see very well, she does not catch on but eventually becomes impatient and decides to cook and eat him anyway. She asks Gretel to climb into the huge oven to see if it is hot enough. Now Gretel acts confused and claims she does not know what to do, so the impatient witch shows her by climbing in. Slam! Gretel shuts the door and the witch burns up while Gretel releases her brother.

They discover riches, jewels, and pearls, so the two children fill their pockets and they find their way home. There they find their father so happy to see them and with all the wealth they bring, they can now live happily ever after. Oh, and the stepmother has died meanwhile. Good riddance, right?

TARGETING AGE LEVEL

This story can appeal to a wide range of young people, and it raises serious issues for adults to confront as well. In the thematic suggestions discussed later, choose to follow the themes raised by your participants. This story provides ample grist for teen and adult conversation about poverty, privilege, and feminism as well as themes for younger children.

READING PLAN

The plot of *Hansel and Gretel* is well known. It captures a range of emotions and adventures: being abandoned, the resourcefulness of children, the dark forest, a witch, candy and cake, and ultimate triumph. This tale invites a likewise broad range of philosophical questions to ponder, some of them quite dark and sinister for a very young child. We find in this story parents abandoning their children, cannibalism, poverty, and lying. Dark themes indeed. Does this tale depict the desperation of people living on the edge and what that can make people do?

When doing philosophy with children and young people, the best way to avoid imposing ideas on them for which they may not be ready is to follow their lead. What interested them in this story? What bothered them? In our themes below, you will find suggested opportunities to approach this story which might appeal to young children, teens, and even an adult discussion group. *Hansel and Gretel* reminds us that fairy tales were originally told in a mixed group of all ages with each listener taking from the story what they found of import.

THEMES

Poverty

We are told that times are desperate for the woodcutter's family. There is barely any food in the house. Poverty is a fact of life for many children in our communities, sometimes even communities that appear on the surface as wealthy or would be deemed wealthy by global standards. There are many institutions that measure and study poverty. One of them is sponsored by the University of Wisconsin: https://www.irp.wisc.edu. Teens and adults may wish to do some reading about poverty before tackling this topic. The discussion plan here invites participants to think about the meaning of poverty and how it affects every aspect of our lives.

Discussion Questions

1. The family in *Hansel and Gretel* is described as poor. What are some of the characteristics of poverty? List them on a sheet of paper or on the board and rank them in order of importance or seriousness.
2. Is poverty different for an adult and a child? If yes, how so?
3. What are the signs of an area where poverty is common?
4. Can someone be poor but happy?
5. Can someone be rich and unhappy?
6. Do other people have an obligation to help those who are really poor? Explain your response. Could abandoning a child be the right thing to do? Why or why not?

Activity

If working with older children, have members of the group research how poverty is measured in our country or in their community. Invite them to share what they learned in a Socratic circle and engage in discussing the following ideas (among others):

- The markers of poverty
- The causes of poverty
- Social justice obligations
- Community responsibilities and opportunities
- Concept of abandonment and what resources might be offered to counteract this practice

Being Resourceful

Hansel is clever and fills his pockets with white stones so that they can leave a trail to help them return home. He is being resourceful and planning for the future.

There are many stories which praise people who are resourceful. The Leo Leoni picture book, *Frederick*, comes to mind. This is a story of mice saving up food for the winter months but one of them, Frederick, appears not to be doing any work at all. When the cold comes, they eat through their stores and Frederick contributes by using his observations of the summer months to paint pictures for the mice to remind them of better times. His contributions to their welfare are stories that turn out to be invaluable to their survival—in addition to their food.

Sometimes being resourceful can take a creative turn. Is resourcefulness always a valuable asset or could it be used for bad? Could you be a resourceful thief or liar?

Discussion Questions

1. Being resourceful implies you can think quickly to solve a problem. What words from below come to mind when you think of a resourceful person?

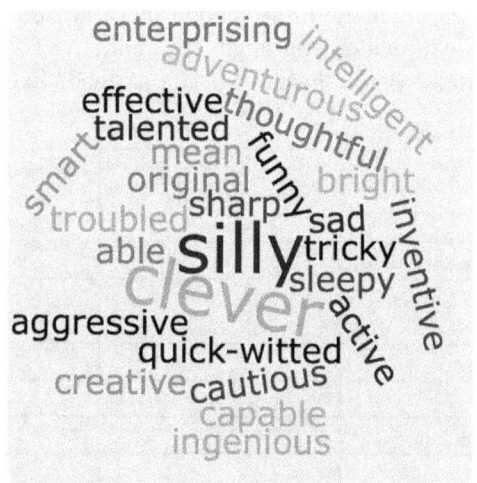

Figure 14.2
Credit Line: Alice V. Gerhardstein

1. How is Hansel resourceful in the story?
2. How is Gretel resourceful in the story?
3. Are other characters resourceful? In each case, describe how the character is resourceful and whether you see this as a good or bad form of being resourceful.
4. Are you being resourceful if you
   a. steal a cookie?
   b. share your homework with the friend?
   c. clean your room?
   d. tie your shoes with a double knot?
   e. help your friend remember where she left her toy?
   f. offer to help to clean the board in exchange for a snack?
5. We are resourceful when we think of a solution to a problem and do so in a way that works. Can you offer an example of a time when you were resourceful?
6. Could someone be resourceful but for a bad goal?
7. Is being resourceful always a desirable action?

Activity

1. Hansel is smart or clever in quickly figuring out how the children can find their way home when he goes out at night and picks up pebbles. This is called being "resourceful." He is able to solve a problem in a new and effective way and quickly. From among the following fairy tale stories and characters with which you might be familiar, are the lead characters resourceful? And if yes, is this good or not so good? Explain your choice.

Fairy tale story	How the character is resourceful?	Good resourcefulness or bad resourcefulness? Why?
Jack in *Jack and the Beanstalk*		
The stepmother in *Hansel and Gretel*		
The Little Mermaid		
Sleeping Beauty		
Rumpelstiltskin in that tale		
The frog in the Frog King		

2. List the main ingredients in describing someone as resourceful. Is it a feeling, a way of thinking, an action, a virtue or vice, or a result obtained? List these on a piece of paper and share with others in the group to compare answers. Which combination seems to capture the best ideas behind being resourceful?

Brothers and Sisters

This story illustrates the close relationship between a brother and sister. In the beginning of the story, it is Hansel who is clever and protects the two, but in the end, Gretel saves the day by being resourceful herself. A sibling is a special kind of relationship, one that might ask more of us that other relationships might. Children often have siblings, so thinking about that relationship can be an important opportunity for them.

Discussion Questions

1. Are Hansel and Gretel like one another? How can you tell?
2. Do you have any sisters or brothers? If yes, are they younger or older? Share your response with the group.
3. Do siblings always have the same last names?

4. Could siblings have the same first name?
5. Can a brother and sister be a friend? Why yes or no?
6. What is the difference between family and friends?
7. What do we owe our older siblings?
8. What do we owe our younger siblings?

Activity

1. Draw a family tree for your family. Who would you put on your tree? Would you include pets? What makes a family?

Forests

Fairy tales often take place in foreboding forests. For the medieval world, forests were places that were the opposite of safety and community. While the town or village represented humanity, community, and safety, forests represented wild nature, the non-human, and danger. They were dark, possibly full of predators, with no roads; they were places of endless confusion with the potential for being lost.

In some feudal states, forests were owned by the gentry and off limits to peasants and others as the lords saw these wild groves as resources for hunting. In some cases, forests were the homes for outcasts from villages and anyone who lived alone was viewed suspiciously. Why would they not want the companionship of other humans to ward off the dark forces of night and disorder? This led many to see forest dwellers as witches or evil spirits. It is no accident that Hansel and Gretel's parents take them into a forest to lose them.

But today we see forests as beautiful outposts of a more benign natural world and we treasure them. Rare in our urban and suburban communities, we treasure opportunities to hike through local woods on trails or visit national parks. With compasses and now GPS devices, we are seldom lost in the woods, although that can still happen in vast tracks of forests in national parks.

Some cultures see forests as a rare chance to regain our humanity by immersing ourselves in the woods, the sounds, smells, and sights of the non-human world. *Shinrin yoku* is Japanese for "forest bathing"—a practice of walking and mediating within a forest grove. (See further resources at the end of the chapter.)

Children can appreciate the terror of being lost in woods with no directions or sense of how to get out even as they might also relish the chances to play among trees and greet woodland animals.

Discussion Questions

1. Hansel and Gretel were lost in the woods. What characteristics make forests or woods scary?
2. Are there characteristics of woods or forests that can make them fun or enjoyable?
3. What kinds of animals live in forests?
4. How many different kinds of forests are there?
5. Why might it be important to preserve natural woodlands in our communities?

Activity

Work in teams to explore what makes a particular kind of forest a community. Use a web or library search to learn about different types of forests to discover their characteristics and how humans interact with them. Create a poster and present it to your class or family.

Being Lost

One of the key themes in this story is being lost. The parents worry that with no food, their entire family will starve and be lost. But the main focus is on losing the children in the forest. It takes two attempts before the parents are successful in abandoning their children.

One of the scariest experiences for a child is to feel lost, whether in the grocery store or out with others. Being lost conveys a deep sense of insecurity and fear: Who cares about me? Where am I? Where am I going? A sense of being lost is a negative relationship to the unknown, the unfamiliar.

Teens and adults alike can experience the feeling of being lost, even when they know where they are physically. But being lost can also lead to adventure. We are out of our element and must explore new regions, geographically, emotionally, or mentally. There are articles, blogs, and books about the benefits of being lost. (For some examples, see the resources at end of this chapter.) To meander around a strange city can provide new experiences and spark creative thinking. But at the same time, we must be alert to the very fact that we are lost and may not understand that which surrounds us.

Discussion Questions

1. Hansel and Gretel are abandoned in the woods and are lost. Have you ever been lost?
2. Could you be lost if you can find your way back home, such as Hansel and Gretel did?

3. Describe your feelings when you were lost.
4. Could you be lost but know where you are?
5. Could you be lost but happy at the same time? How so or why not?
6. What is the similarity and difference between being lost in science class and being lost in your neighborhood?
7. Is experiencing a loss the same as being lost? Why yes or no?
8. What is the worst thing about being lost? What is the best thing?

Activity

In the following chart, mark whether you think the example is a good one of being lost and why or why not. Add your own examples for discussion.

The event or example	Are you lost?	Why yes or no	If lost, type described
At the mall, you cannot find your parent			
The teacher is going over the math homework			
Your friends go out without inviting you			
You are immersed in reading your favorite book			
Your best friend speaks Spanish but you know only a few words			
Your mom gets on the subway train but the doors close before you can get on			

Witches

Witches feature prominently in some classic fairy tales. We think of *Sleeping Beauty*, *Snow White*, and certainly *Hansel and Gretel*. For many children, the image of a witch may come from the classic movie *The Wizard of Oz*, where Margaret Hamilton wears all black, is ugly and green of complexion, and has that tall pointed hat. The witch costume for Halloween echoes this depiction.

Then again, we also meet Glenda, the beautiful witch. With the Harry Potter series, children gained new images of what a witch might look like and in many cases they could be admired. And shows featuring teenage witches are now recasting the vision of a witch into a somewhat cool persona.

Most witches in children's stories are old, ugly, and women living on the outskirts of civilization; they are outcasts from the community and are viewed as evil. Surprisingly this captures part of the aura of being a witch in previous centuries. They were often women who lived without a man, were independent, were healers, and therefore practiced "magic." They may have had animal companions who were transformed into evil spirits by the imagination and fear of the townspeople. This reveals the deep-seated prejudices and fears of earlier times against women who could make their own decisions and were not under the rule of a man.

In *Hansel and Gretel*, however, the witch is a cannibal and clearly an evil being who threatens the very life of the children. She also represents the dangers to children when they stray from their parents and their home. The forest is indeed a foreboding place where evil beings lurk, ready to snatch unsuspecting innocents, and destroy them.

Discussion Questions

1. Describe what you think the witch in *Hansel and Gretel* looks like.
2. What character traits does this witch show in her actions?
3. How do you think this witch became the way she is described in the story?
4. What makes a witch different from other women?
5. Can a man be a witch?
6. How could we tell if someone is a witch?
7. Is being a witch always bad? Could there be good witches? If yes, are they still witches?
8. If there is no such thing as a witch, can we still describe them and talk about them?

Activity

1. Complete the following sentences which asks you to describe a witch. Create circles on the board or on large pieces of paper and write in all the answers from the group.

   Witches look like _____.
   Witches sound like _____.
   Witches smell like _____.
   Witches love _____.
   Witches hate _____.
   Witches do _____.

Did you all come up with the same answers? Discuss what each person contributed.

Do only witches have these characteristics?

Must witches have these characteristics?

2. Read about the Salem witch trials. (See resources at the end of the chapter.) Were the accused really witches? Why do you think yes or no?

Stealing

It might be worth noting that the children steal from the witch before she invites them in and they lie about it. They start eating her house and then claim that a mouse is nibbling at the house. Of course, they are starving but are they not still stealing? Can stealing ever be justified? We often leap to the example of a man stealing a loaf of bread to feed his starving family but (1) is this not still stealing and (2) what about the person from whom he is stealing? What if this is their livelihood?

Discussion Questions

1. Did Hansel and Gretel steal from the witch when they started to eat her house?
2. What makes stealing wrong?
3. Can stealing ever be right? Why yes or why no?
4. Does it matter what you are stealing?
5. Does it matter from whom you are stealing?
6. If someone steals from you, is it OK to steal from them?
7. If you steal from someone, is it OK if they steal from you?

Activity

Discuss the examples in the following chart and add you own.

Item to steal	Is it wrong?	Why yes or no? Give reasons	Questions to ask
A wallet with money			
My heart			
Answers to a quiz			
Answers to a big exam			
Food to eat			
Cheap bracelet from a store			

Item to steal	Is it wrong?	Why yes or no? Give reasons	Questions to ask
First base in a ball game			
The car keys from a friend			
Your neighbor's dog whom he is abusing			

Playing Tricks

Hansel and Gretel might be said to be playing tricks on the old woman. Hansel holds out a chicken bone when the witch asks to feel his finger to check if he is fattening up. And Gretel pretends she does not understand how to check the oven so that the witch climbs in to show her but then she quickly slams the door closed and cooks the witch.

We play tricks on people for all sorts of reasons. Sometimes we do it out of affection or love. Sometimes we do it out of spite, dislike, or a desire to get someone in trouble. Is playing a trick the same as playing a game? Is it equivalent to lying or misrepresenting something? Are we manipulating people unfairly when we play tricks on them? Or, is that simply a gesture of humor and as suggested above, simply a sign of friendship or comfortableness with a person.

It would appear that to gauge whether playing a trick on someone is a bad or good action requires a lot of information about intention, outcome, the agents and patients involved, and the situation.

Discussion Questions

1. Were Hansel and Gretel playing tricks on the witch when they were her captive? How so or why not?
2. Can you offer an example of playing a trick on someone? Make a list of what you come up with.
3. What makes playing a trick a fun action?
4. When might playing a trick be wrong?
5. Does it matter why you decided to play a trick on someone when determining whether it is nice or not?
6. Does it matter as to whom you played the trick to determine that?
7. If someone treats you badly, is it OK to play a trick on them?
8. How is playing a trick like and unlike playing a game?

Loyalty

Hansel and Gretel are loyal to one another and ultimately to their parents as they return home after escaping from the witch, even though they know their parents had abandoned them. Loyalty between siblings and among family members runs deep. The close relationship of family counts far more than even our best friends. But should there be limits to loyalty? Should we be loyal to a parent—or anyone—who hurts us? While loyalty might be viewed as a classic virtue, we can learn from Aristotle in that virtues can often morph into vices if carried to an extreme.

Discussion Questions

1. How are Hansel and Gretel loyal to one another?
2. Are they also loyal to their parents?
3. How would you define loyalty? Pick three words that seem to describe what loyalty is and share them with others.
4. To what or whom do we owe loyalty?
5. Can you be loyal to an animal? To a tree or house?
6. Should there be limits to our loyalty? Try the chart below and discuss.
7. What makes someone a loyal citizen? Employee? Friend?
8. Are there degrees of loyalty, and, if yes, how do we determine what they are?

Activity [Adapt if you wish to use this with younger children.]

Consider these examples and mark whether the person is being loyal and why or why not. Should they be loyal?

Scenario	Is the character being loyal?	Should they be loyal?	Explain your answer
Rob's little sister is being made fun of on the bus and he tells the other kids to leave her alone.			
Lucy's best friend asks her to lie for her to cover that she was not at your house last night. Lucy refuses to cover for her.			

Scenario	Is the character being loyal?	Should they be loyal?	Explain your answer
John sees his co-workers take some money from the cash register but their boss is always so mean to them. He keeps quiet since no one else saw this anyway.			
Magda's parents are vegetarians and insist that their family avoid meat but when she is out to dinner with friends, the hamburgers look delicious. Magda decides to eat one so that her friends do not feel bad.			
Dale cheats on his math exam because it was a horrible night at home with his parents arguing. His parents are both overanxious that he gets into a really top college and this may be an important test for his final grade.			
Joaquin has been best friends with Marlo since kindergarten but the new kid in school seems supernice and he would like to hang out with him instead of Mario.			

SOURCES TO CONSULT FOR MORE INFORMATION

On forest bathing: Shirin Yoku: http://www.shinrin-yoku.org/shinrin-yoku.html
On types of forests: https://www.zmescience.com/other/did-you-know/different-types-forests/

On being lost: http://www.grandcanyonwriter.com/2016/04/the-benefits-of-being-lost.html

Solnit, Rebecca. *A Field Guide to Getting Lost*. New York: Penguin Books, 2006.

A blog post on the advantages of being lost: https://www.andymort.com/get-lost/

On the Salem Witch trials

From the Smithsonian: https://www.smithsonianmag.com/history/a-brief-history-of-the-salem-witch-trials-175162489/

From the History channel: https://www.history.com/topics/colonial-america/salem-witch-trials

The Encyclopedia Britannica online: https://www.britannica.com/event/Salem-witch-trials

Chapter 15

Snow White

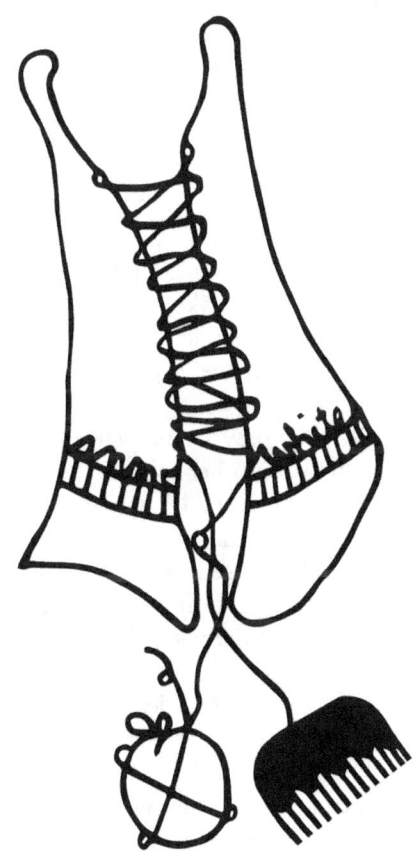

Figure 15.1
Credit Line: Alice V. Gerhardstein

Chapter 15

PLOT

This fairy tale is well known to American audiences, mostly through the classic Disney version. But the Grimms' retelling does offer some variations that merit exploration. Their version opens with a queen contemplating the snow outside her window and when she pricks her finger a drop of deep red blood falls on the snow. She wishes "for a child as white as snow, as red as blood, and as black as the wood of the widow frame." When her daughter is born she names her "Snow White" and then promptly dies.

Her husband remarries and his new wife spends a lot of time staring into her magic mirror checking on the status of her beauty. The mirror always claims her to be the fairest in the land until one day the mirror signals that little Snow White has surpassed the queen in beauty. This leads the queen into a jealous fury, and she commands a huntsman to take the child into the woods and kill it, bringing back her lungs and liver for the queen to eat. As the huntsman is about to fulfill his task, the little girl begs for her life and promises to leave. He takes pity on her and kills a boar instead, returning to the castle with the liver and lungs which the queen cooks and eats.

Meanwhile, Snow White wanders scared and alone in the dark forest until she comes across a little house. When she enters, she finds it spic and span clean and the table is set for seven. She nibbles a bit off of each plate and drinks a drop from each cup. Exhausted, she falls asleep in one of the beds. Seven dwarfs return home and discover her and take pity on her because of her beauty. The next morning they strike a bargain: Snow White will serve as their housekeeper and they will let her live with them. As they know her story, they warn her to not let anyone in during the day lest the evil stepmother tries to kill her again.

Of course, Snow White falls prey to the plans of the stepmother. When checking on her beauty status with her mirror, the stepmother learns with horror that Snow White is still alive and living in the cottage with the dwarfs. Off she goes, disguised as an old peddler woman. On the first visit, she convinces Snow White to let her in and sells her stays. These are cords that were used to pull in a corset to give a girl a tiny waist. Snow White invites her in and lets her lace up the stays, but the wicked queen pulls them so tight that she passes out.

The dwarfs arrive home and think she is dead but upon cutting the cords, she comes back to life. Again they sternly warn her about strangers, but the next day the old lady is back selling a comb. Again she lets her in and as soon as the woman puts the poisoned comb in her hair, Snow White falls down seemingly dead. The dwarfs return and remove the comb, again saving her life.

On the third try, the queen is very devious and poisons an apple in such a way that she offers to share it with the girl who gladly accepts the gift.

A piece of the apple touches her lips, and before she can swallow it, Snow White collapses. This time the dwarfs judge that she has died and they put her in a glass casket. However, Snow White does not lose her pink cheeks so they keep the casket for a long time.

One day a prince comes upon the casket and is so taken with her beauty that he begs the dwarfs to let him take her. One of his servants carrying the casket stumbles and jostles the casket enough to dislodge the piece of apple from her mouth. Snow White returns to life and immediately agrees to marry the prince. At her wedding the wicked queen shows up to see who this newest rival to her beauty might be but is forced to put on iron slippers that were heated in the fire and dance until she dies.

READING PLAN

While this story appeals to all ages, it might be interesting to introduce it to older children and teens so as to explore some of the very problematic issues that it raises. The reader could bill this as "Snow White: a feminist challenge" or indicate that there are some serious subtexts or problems to be found in this tale.

The questions suggested below are designed for young people who might enjoy interrogating some of the societal roles we face today brought to the fore by this classic tale.

However, if you share this tale with younger children, you can still find opportunities to explore these themes in ways that will puzzle, delight, and get them thinking.

THEMES

Beauty and Its Price

While the queen stepmother is the villain here, she is desperate to keep her status as the most beautiful. We might mock her for her vanity and envy, but we can also acknowledge our own emphasis on youth and beauty and the way in which women become invisible. Teens come into their power with their youth and beauty but even they can suffer greatly if they do not measure up to the strict and narrow definition of female beauty and male appearance.

We are constantly being bombarded by images and messages that promise us success and happiness if we look a certain way: thin; well-dressed; and with perfect skin, hair, and teeth. While we are aware of the absurdity of these pressures and the power that photoshop wields to seduce us into feeling inadequate, we still fall under the spell of these messages. We find even kindergartners worried about their weight and how they look.

And while children and teens know the right things to say (It only matters how beautiful you are inside! And beauty is only skin deep), they have internalized these impossible standards and measure themselves as failing in too many ways.

Discussion Questions

1. The queen spends a lot of time asking her mirror who is the fairest? Why do you think she does this?
2. Is being beautiful important for us today? If yes, how so? If not, why not?
3. What images of beauty do you see in the media today?
4. What is the same and what is different among a beautiful baby, a beautiful teen, a beautiful fifty years old and a beautiful ninety years old? Can all of these be beautiful, and if yes, how so?
5. What does the phrase "beauty is only skin deep" mean?
6. What does the phrase "She is beautiful in the inside" mean? Would we ask the same question of a boy or young man? Why or why not?

Project: Our Images of Beauty

Go through magazines, scan TV and movies, and other media for examples of beauty. Look for implicit standards of beauty and list them on a poster or simply on one shared list. Fairy tales often message the power of beauty—as we see here in *Snow White*. Is beauty power? Should it be power?

Project: Beauty Changes

Research how our notions of beauty has changed over time and across cultures. What might beauty signify in different eras and different places?

Cannibalism

In this version of *Snow White*, the stepmother desires to eat the liver and lungs of Snow White and insists that the huntsman, after killing her, bring them back for her. This rings particularly gruesome to us today. Why did she choose those two internal organs? Why is eating one's own kind so repellant to us even as just a concept? This may be a theme best saved for older teens and adults but it merits some attention.

While we tend to relegate cannibalism to a tribal past or even further back in time, there have been instances where humans did resort to eating one another. Two examples are the Donner Party which was stranded for months in the snowy Sierra Nevada mountains in the 1840s and in 1972 a plane crash in the Andes led some young men to cannibalism, again for survival. Perhaps these are quite different scenarios? Can cannibalism be justified in some situations, and if yes, what would the criteria be for that?

Discussion Questions

1. The queen in this version of our fairy tale wants to eat the lungs and liver of Snow White. What might be her motive?
2. Why might be some of the reasons we find cannibalism such a taboo practice today?
3. Is there anything inherently wrong with eating someone whom we did not kill? Why yes or why no?
4. There are "life-boat scenarios" in which we are asked to rank individuals in terms of survival value. Should we really do this, and if yes, how can we be fair?
5. Can we judge others for practices that they might find familiar and acceptable? If yes, on what grounds? If no, could this ever be challenged?

Research Project: Debating Cannibalism

There have been famous instances of cannibalism for survival, the Donner Party in the 1840s and a group of men whose plane crashed in the 1970s. Find a case where cannibalism might be understood as acceptable and explore the situation, the individuals involved, and the decisions they had to make.

Create a case to debate as to the ethics of the situation, looking at all agents, the circumstances, and possible justifications for different courses of action. What if the practices go back to an indigenous societal beliefs about eating one's enemies? Would this too be legitimate or might we be able to argue against such practices and beliefs?

Women's/Men's Roles

While many fairy tales depict young women as waiting to be rescued, *Snow White* might be read as particularly egregious in terms of setting up gender roles. We have the jealous older woman who wants to get rid of her rival for beauty, the vapid, and apparently not too bright young beauty herself who is assigned typical women's tasks as serving as the housekeeper, and the prince who rescues her and chooses to marry a passive sleeping girl simply because she is beautiful.

While we love to enjoy the drama of this story and the happy ending, we might want to take a close look at the subtext messaging here to young girls and to boys. Does this tale set up expectations that girls need rescuing and that it is the job of boys to make decisions and save those girls?

Discussion Questions

1. What positions and roles do you find for women and men in this classic fairy tale? Make a list and discuss whether these are familiar to us today.
2. Are there tasks in our culture that are better performed by women or by men? What would they be, if any?
3. Are women better nurturers than men? Why or why not? What characteristics are needed to be good at taking care of others?
4. Are men better at certain jobs or careers than women? Develop your answer with examples and explanations as to why, or why not.
5. Do stories like *Snow White* help children better understand their future roles in society or could they be problematic in some way?
6. Is it such a bad thing that men and women have different roles assigned by gender if that helps the society function well?

Activity

In the following chart, indicate whether a particular task is done more by men or by women and whether both might be able to do it. Add any qualifiers if you wish. And see if you can add some examples at the end.

Type of task or job	More women	More men	Both equally perform this task	Reasons for your choice
Fighting fires in the city				
Nursing				
Being a doctor				
Teaching pre-school children				
Farming a large dairy farm				
Cleaning the house				

Type of task or job	More women	More men	Both equally perform this task	Reasons for your choice
Yard work				
Lifeguard at the beach				
Police officer				
Ballet dancer				
Working as an engineer				
Taking care of babies				

Waiting for the Prince?

At the end of the tale, Snow White is rescued by the prince who falls for her beauty as displayed in the glass coffin. He wants to take the coffin home so that he can continue to view her. Does that sound a bit creepy? We might wish to question this entire scenario! But perhaps this will prompt your young people to write up alternative endings to this tale, or perhaps rewrite the entire story to free both the men and women in it from rigid stereotypes.

Project

How might you rewrite this fairy tale to capture our contemporary views of men, women, gender in general? Work on a creative project:

- A short story which retells *Snow White* but with a modern sensibility
- The plot for a movie updated to present times
- A song or set of songs that might offer an alternative reading of *Snow White*
- Another project of your own creative choosing

Chapter 16

Master Cat or *Puss 'n Boots*

Figure 16.1

Chapter 16

PLOT

This fairy tale is quite problematic. Despite the main character being a sharp-witted and engaging cat, the reader can find lots to question. Cats have not been universally liked and many people still consider them to be sneaky and sly. Our cat here is extraordinary for a couple of reasons: he speaks, he insists on wearing a pair of boots, and he completely dedicates to helping a master who was not so keen on him to begin with.

The version to read is by Charles Perrault who captures the ironic twists of fate and farce exhibited in this tale of a trickster who wins everything for his master. It opens with the death of a simple miller who bequeaths to his three sons his mill, a donkey, and cat—in descending order from oldest to youngest son.

The younger son grumbles that a cat is useless for helping him make a living and all he can imagine to do with it is eat it and make a muff from the fur. The cat overhears this comment and instead of disappearing he offers to help his hapless master become successful. All he asks is a pair of riding boots suitable for a seventeenth-century cavalier and a pouch.

Using his hunting skills, the cat catches a wide range of game and delivers it to the king, each time claiming it is a present from his lord, the Marquis de Carabas. As the gifts continue, the king becomes familiar with the cat and appreciates his generosity, or rather that of his master. Oddly, no one seems to think that a talking cat wearing clothes is strange.

During an outing for the king and his beautiful daughter, they pass by a river where the young peasant man is swimming, at the instructions of his cat. The cat yowls that his master is drowning and the king orders his men to save him. He outfits him with fine clothes and as the king praises him, the daughter finds the young man quite handsome and is smitten.

Invited into the carriage, the young man gets to ride with the beautiful princess and her father while the cat continues his schemes. He threatens a group of mowers to say the field in which they are working belongs to the Marquis and repeats the same ploy with farmers harvesting grain. The king begins to see this young man as quite wealthy and an excellent prospect.

Meanwhile the cat has sprinted ahead to a castle owned by an ogre whose magic allows him to change into anything. The cat tricks him into turning into a lion (scary!) but then into a mouse and as soon as the ogre, showing off his powers, does so, the cat leaps on the mouse and eats him. When the king's entourage arrives, the cat invites them into his master's palace.

As they enjoy a vast meal, the king grandly offers the hand of his daughter to the young man who gladly accepts. As the story ends, the cat lives as a lord and did not have to catch his supper, unless he wished to hunt it himself! The tale concludes with two odd morals: one praises the advantages of being industrious over having inherited riches while the second ironically comments on a poor young man winning the heart of a princess as a thumb in the nose to the rich.

AGE RANGE

This tale is enjoyable for children through teens, and for adults. Depending upon your audience, you may wish to choose different themes to explore, or as recommended, be open to your young person's or group's decision as to what interested them.

READING PLAN

This tale may be familiar to your children but there are many different versions. In some the young man callously kills his helpful cat but in most they end happily. It is a relatively short tale and easy to read together or out loud. This particular fairy tale raises some troubling issues: at what price success? Is deception a good thing if the end result is good?

Your readers may see the cat as a hero but they might also question his motives and his methods. Do we find here a tale of greed and materialism? Does our peasant and princess really live happily ever after? Or, perhaps the cat is simply the lovable trickster figure who takes care of those he likes.

THEMES TO EXPLORE

Deception

This entire story circles around an elaborate con job or act of deception. The cat persistently misrepresents his master to the king, and this campaign pays off big time in the end. Should we condone these actions because . . . well, because we like the hapless young man? Or, we admire the cat for his creativity? Or, maybe we think that anyone who believes a talking cat rather deserves to be deceived. What do your young people think about this?

Discussion Questions

1. How many times does the cat act deceptively in this story? See if you can find them all.
2. Are all acts of deceptions lie?
3. Could you deceive someone by telling the truth? If yes, how so?

4. If you deceive someone for a good cause, does that make it alright? Offer an example and explain why yes or no.
5. Are there people or situations where deception is deserved? If yes, offer a scenario to illustrate?
6. If someone is deceived, are they responsible for not figuring it out or being taken in?

Activity

In the following chart, decide if the action is one of deception or not and if yes, whether it is the wrong thing to do or OK.

Act of deception	Wrong thing to do	OK to do	Your reason
Sue is playing cards with Tom and pretends to be worried so as to trick him into thinking she has a bad hand.			
John is always friendly and polite to his boss to his face but behind his back he is very critical.			
Mary's grandmother is very old and has Alzheimer's. Mary's mom lets her think that her husband, Mary's grandfather, is still alive.			
Dave really needs help with his art project, so he fakes a sprained wrist to have his friend give him some assistance.			
Judy's friend is wearing an outfit that is totally inappropriate for work but Judy compliments her and says she looks great.			
Mike is best friends with Jimmy but decides he really likes Fred better and decides not to say anything to Jimmy about this.			

Friends

The cat appears to be a great friend to his young master. He helps him again and again. In the end, his master rewards him for his assistance by making him a lord. Friends take care of friends, don't they? But do the cat's actions in some way raise troubling questions about friendship? Is he really a friend when he lies again and again, even if it is to help the young man? What do we owe our friends and are there any lines we might establish for the limits of obligation? So how do we determine the extent of obligations to friends when friendships can take so many different forms?

Discussion Questions

1. In this story, the cat acts as a true friend to his young master. Why might this be a surprising act on the part of the cat?
2. What makes someone a friend? List all the characteristics that you think a person needs to be a friend.
3. Can friends be bad friends or are all friendships good? Explain your response.
4. If a friend acts badly on your behalf, are they still your friend? (Maybe the cat is not really a true friend?)
5. Are there different types or degrees of friendship? Make a chart to illustrate your answer.
6. Can we be friends with a cat? Or other animals? Any animal or only some?

Cats

Cats usually get a bad reputation in fairy tales. They are witch's familiars and they eat more defenseless little mice. But here we find a cat as a hero, or is he a kind of anti-hero? Of course, this is not just any cat but a rather magical cat, a cat that can talk and engage in social niceties with kings and peasants. This cat has been thoroughly anthropomorphized, turned into a human-like character. We also find Puss linking two completely separate worlds, that of the lower-class workers like the miller and his sons and the highest aristocratic class in the land, that of the king and his daughter.

What does this reveal about the nature of felines? As a domesticated species, the nature of cats has been actively shaped by humans and their needs and desires. Is this a good or bad thing? And how have cats presented a number of serious ecological issues for us today?

Discussion Questions

1. The hero of the tale clearly appears to be the cat. How is this different from cats of your acquaintance?
2. What makes a cat to be a cat? See if you can find the definition of this animal and its distinguishing characteristics.
3. How have cats and human beings bonded together through history?

4. Do you like to dislike cats? Give reasons for your answer.
5. Many fairy tales feature cats as something to be scared of. Even today, some people are fearful of cats. Why so?
6. While Puss 'n Boots speaks, many people think cats can communicate in their own way. What do you think?
7. Cats can often cause ecological damage to their environment. How so? Should this change how we act toward cats?
8. If cats are simply acting catlike, can we blame them if they kill songbirds or hurt small creatures?

Project

If you are working with older students, have them do research projects on the effects of domesticated felines on the environment. They are particularly pernicious against song birds. Have your young people create posters about cats:

- their history
- the variety of breeds
- how they help human beings
- but also the environmental impact they have and possible solutions
- the questions that cats provoke

Share the posters with students or see if there are opportunities to share with the public via a library or philosophy club.

Lying

Lying is a particular form of deception which entails a person saying something that they know to be untrue to another person with the intention of having them believe it. As suggested above, we may lie sometimes to help another person. But is lying ever justified? What criteria would we use to condemn lying in all cases or perhaps to allow it as a justified action in some? And is all lying verbal? Can I lie in not speaking? Or, through some communication expressed bodily but not verbally?

Discussion Questions

1. In our tale, the cat tells many lies to deceive the king and his court. How many lies can you find in this story?
2. Can you lie to someone and not know you are doing it?
3. Could a lie be the right thing to do? Explain.
4. Why do we so often see lying as a bad thing to do?

5. Can you lie without saying anything? Give an example.
6. What makes a lie to be a lie? List all the necessary criteria from the list below:

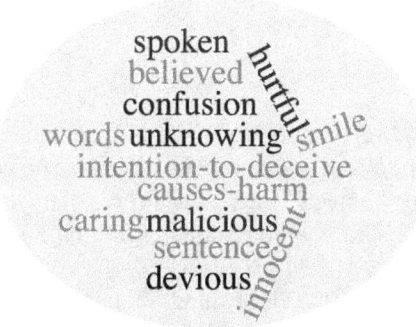

Figure 16.2

7. If no one believes what you are saying, are you still lying?

Success and What Matters

One of the key themes in this story is the path to success. The young man rues that he has been given nothing by his father to help him be successful in life. But the cat works very hard to change that. What vision of success do we find in this story? To what extent does it sound very familiar to our own models of success? Do we find anything to question about the importance of love, wealth, fine things, and status?

Discussion Questions

1. From what you can find in this story, what does the young man think he wants in life?
2. The king is much impressed by the cat's lord, based on the supposed gifts from him and the cat's comments. What makes him like the young man before he has even seen him?
3. What appears to be important values for the following characters:
   - The cat
   - The young man
   - The king
   - His princess daughter

4. Why did each character seek out the value they did? Explain your own interpretation of the tale here.
  5. To what extent are these values and goals still important today?
  6. If you could choose only one goal or one thing to value, what would it be and why? Compare your answers to those of others.

Materialism

Materialism has a bad reputation. It sounds as if someone is shallow and obsessed with having more and more material objects. And yet we can longingly seek out these glittery objects. Certainly, in this fairy tale, the focus is on owning land, a castle, and winning the hand of a high-status princess—who is beautiful as well.

While we might all say the right thing about how none of these are important, it is worth noting that not only in fairy tales are material possessions the ultimate sign of success and the good life but in our own world as well. We continually are bombarded with ads for this or that next thing that will guarantee that we too shall "live happily ever after," if we purchase whatever is being touted.

One way to get to the heart of materialism is to explore what material good we genuinely need to be happy. Despite the lofty-sounding platitude that all we need is love, we do in fact need some key material goods to live a happy and fulfilling life. Not all materials are bad.

Discussion Questions

  1. In our tale the young man ends up with many riches. What are they?
  2. What things do you have that are very important to have? Why are they so?
  3. What would you like to have? Make a list of your top five choices.
  4. Make a list of three things you have that you would not miss if you lost them.
  5. We sometimes make a distinction between things we want and things we need. Mark your first list with a "W" if you think this is something you want and an "N" if you think this is something you need.

Activity

In the following chart, choose whether the object is something you think you need or want, or both, and explain why you chose the category you did.

Object	Need?	Want?	Both	Reasons
New outfit				
Bicycle				
Pen				
Food				
Friends				
A pet				
A job				
Water				
Medicine				
Fame				
High grade in math				

Discuss your responses with others to see why you chose different categories or agreed on the same ones.

Intentions/Consequences

Our tale features the cat doing lots of potentially bad things but for an apparently selfless reason, to help his master. Then again, could the cat anticipate a nice reward for his help and be motivated by that? Sometimes one's intentions matter far more than the results of one's actions—but not always. Should we be bothered by the means used by our feline hero or simply be happy for the young man whose cat's machinations result in his winning everything?

Many a trickster figure is a lovable scoundrel who does terrible things either for a good cause or to pay back someone who deserves it. Should that matter? Then again, was the cat mostly concerned with his young owner or his own welfare?

Discussion Questions

1. What intentions does each character in this story reveal regarding their actions?
2. The cat tricks the ogre and ends up eating him. Is this a good or bad action and why?
3. If you have good intentions, does that matter more than what follows from your decisions? Offer examples to illustrate your response.
4. Can we always know people's intentions in acting?
5. Can we know our own intentions in making decisions?
6. How important is it to know one's intention before judging and acting?

Activity

Offer stories or scenarios which illustrate the various combinations from the options listed here. What does this tell us about judging the morality of decisions?

Intention	Outcome: bad	Outcome: good
Good intentions		
Bad intentions		
Uncertain intentions		

Chapter 17

The Story of the Three Little Bears

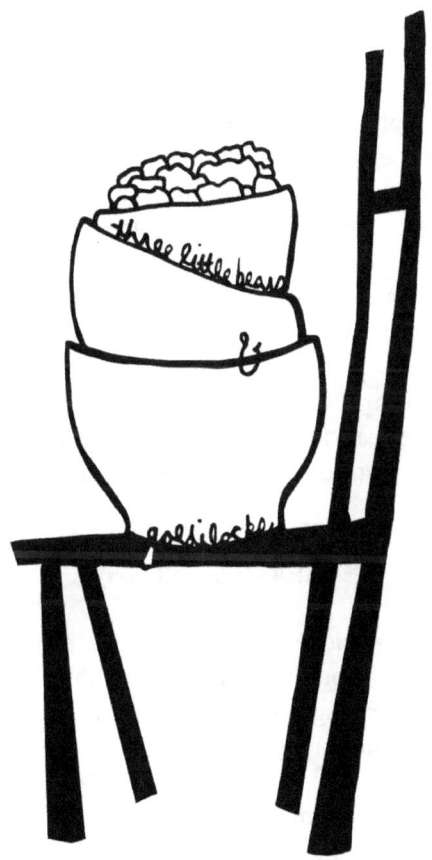

Figure 17.1

PLOT

This beloved and very familiar fairy tale features animals and, of course, a little girl named Goldilocks. We meet the three bears: sometimes they are described as mama, papa, and baby bear. In other versions, they are a wee or small bear, a middle-sized bear, and a huge bear. Each bear has their plates and cups, their chairs, and their beds designed to fit them.

One day after their breakfast was set on the table, the three decide to go for a walk to let the porridge cool. While they were out, a little girl shows up at their door and looks in the window, peeps in the keyhole, and seeing no one, turns the handle and enters. Upon entering, she spies the porridge and decides to try it. The big bear's was too hot, the middle bear's was too cold, but the little bear's was just right. When she tried out the chairs, the big bear's was too hard, the middle bear's was too soft, but again, the wee bear's was perfect—until she falls through the seat! She makes her way upstairs and tries out all three beds with pretty much the patterned result. In one version, they are too hard, too soft, just right but in another telling, the head is too high in the big bear's, too high at the foot for the middle bear, but just right in the wee bear's bed and she falls asleep.

When the bears return, they go through the cycle of each one noticing that someone has tried their porridge and sat in their chairs. The little bear wails that his porridge is gone and his chair broken. When they proceed upstairs, they see their beds have been mussed up but find the offending little girl asleep in the little bear's bed. Goldilocks wakes up and jumps out the window, running home, we presume.

In some versions of this story, we find moralistic comments all along the way: how trusting the bears are and how rude is Goldilocks, in and what good behavior the bears demonstrate compared to the intruder.

READING PLAN

We find our bears to be looking and acting quite human and the pattern of threes is repeated throughout the story. Indeed, this story is clearly a story which benefits from reading out loud and includes a repetitive chorus of events. This particular story might be perfect for younger children, both as it is so familiar, has a lyrical repetitive nature which is appealing, and yet still raises some great points for philosophical inquiry. The following themes and activities are particularly targeted for younger children but of course can be used with older ones as well.

THEMES

Animals and People

This story introduces us to three bears who act very much like people. They live in a house, have chairs and beds, and communicate much as humans do. While animals do not normally live as we do, they nevertheless have elemental needs parallel to our own. Perhaps your children will be interested in exploring how animals live.

Discussion Questions

1. Do the animals in this story sound like real bears? Why or why not?
2. Do bears have houses? If yes, what kind?
3. Do bears eat porridge? What do bears eat?
4. Do bears use beds? What kind of beds?
5. What are some of the ways that animals live like us?
6. What are some of the ways that animals live differently from us?

Activity

Have the children come up with a list of animals and then explore the following aspects of that animal's life:

- What kind of house or shelter they need
- What they eat
- What tools they use
- How they communicate with one another

Consider making a poster or collage of each animal's "life style."

Curiosity and Manners

Goldilocks is a curious little girl. Curiosity is a good quality to have in most cases. But has she gone too far? How do we decide when curiosity becomes something undesirable? When is it dangerous? Intrudes on others? Is Goldilocks showing good manners by being curious?

Discussion Questions

1. Goldilocks is interested in the house in the woods and wants to know what is in it. Is she being curious?

2. What does it mean to be curious? What kinds of things would you do or say to show that you were curious?
3. Is curiosity a good thing to have? Why yes or no?
4. Can you be too curious? Why?
5. We tend to think of curiosity as a good quality to have? Could it be a vice? Why or when might it be a bad quality to have?
6. Could being curious show bad manners? Why yes or no?
7. What are manners?
8. Who showed better manners, Goldilocks or the bears? Why did you choose one over the other?
9. There is a saying, "Curiosity killed the cat and satisfaction brought it back." What do you think that means?

Activity on Manners

Invite your children to fill in the following chart and discuss their responses. Have them add some examples of their own.

Manners	Bad manners?	Good manners?	Neither/ not sure	Your explanation
Finishing everything on your plate				
Burping at the table				
Saying 'excuse me' before you speak				
Covering your mouth when you cough				
Telling your mother when your baby brother is mean to you				
Speaking when your teacher is talking				
Getting up and walking around the classroom				
Pushing another child off the swings because it is your turn				
Asking your teacher about his girlfriend				

Numbers and the Theme of Three

This fairy tale is full of repetition and patterns of three. Perhaps, the children will want to track or make note of how many times things or events happen in threes.

Discussion Questions

1. What number seems to show up a lot in this story?
2. How many times can you find groups of three?
3. Do you have a favorite number? If yes, what is it? What makes it your favorite?
4. Where do numbers come from?
5. Are numbers real or do we simply think or say them?
6. Where do you use numbers?

Getting Things Just Right

In this fairy tale we find the number three used to set up relationships between three possibilities: bowls of porridge, chairs, and beds. The contrasts are paralleled: one is too much, the second is not enough, and the third is just right, that is, the happy medium. This theme is somewhat reminiscent of Aristotle's theory of virtue where the right way to be is a middle or mean between two extremes, one of excess and the other of deficit. Perhaps your group will want to pursue this calculation of "just right" to see how it appears in their own lives.

Discussion Questions

1. When Goldilocks tries each bear's dish, chair, or bed, she describes them in what ways?
2. Can you give examples of things which are too much? Others which are not enough?
3. How do we decide what is "just right"?

Activity

In the following chart, ask the children to identify which item is too much of some quality and which is too little. Should any of them be labeled as just right?

Example: compared to you, how would you label the following?	Too much	Too little	Just right	Your explanation
A whole gallon of milk to drink with your lunch				
A pair of shoes that fit a Barbie doll for you to wear to school				
You tell a joke and your friends laugh				
You and your family go for a ten-mile hike				
You and your family take the dog for a walk around your block				
You show how brave you are by screaming at your teacher that she is wrong				
You show how brave you are by asking a question in class when prompted to do so				
You show how brave you are by not saying anything when asked who spilled the juice, even though you know				

Appendix A

For More Information about Philosophy and Children

If this is your first foray into philosophical inquiry, you might want to explore some of the excellent books on this topic. There are a growing number of books and online sources for supporting philosophical inquiry with children. Here are some of the best along with brief commentary but more are being published every year.

Hannan, Patricia and Echeverria, Eugenio. *Philosophy with Teenagers*. New York: Continuum, 2009.
This is a particularly useful source if you are working with teens. Hannan and Echeverria are experienced facilitators in philosophical dialogue and have presented workshops and published extensively in the field.

Lipman, Matthew, Ann Margaret Sharp, and Frederick S. Oscanyan, *Philosophy in the Classroom*. Philadelphia, PA: Temple University Press, 1980.
While this text may look old, it is the classic statement of what philosophy looks like in the classroom and why education needs philosophical dialogue for children of all ages. Lipman and Sharp were pioneers in the promulgation of philosophy for children and young people and created many philosophical novels to be used with young people and the theoretical foundation behind the movement.

Matthew, Gareth, *Philosophy and the Young Child*. Boston, MA: Harvard University Press, 1980.
Matthew, Gareth, *Dialogues*. Boston, MA: Harvard University Press, 1992.
Gareth Matthews was likewise an early proponent for having philosophical conversation with children. Both of these texts are easy and engaging and offer lots of examples of children thinking philosophically. These

examples can help you "tune your ear" to recognize philosophical potential in children's comments and questions.

McCall, Catherine, *Transforming Thinking—Philosophical Inquiry in the Primary and Secondary Classroom*. New York: Routledge, 2009.
McCall's text is more theoretical but she offers an excellent guide for developing genuine philosophical thinking and dialogue among children. She reminds us that this is not simply about chatting or accepting all answers as wonderful. She also explains how her method differs from that of others.

Mohr Lone, Jana, *The Philosophical Child*. Lanham, MD: Rowman & Littlefield, 2012.
Mohr Lone, the founder and past president of PLATO, an American organization dedicated to promoting philosophy with children and young people, offers a wonderful invitation to parents and others to try philosophy with the children in their lives. An experienced facilitator herself, she has written many articles and other books, but this is a great choice for parents.

Stanley, Sara, *Why Think? Philosophical Play from 3–11*. New York: Continuum, 2012.
Stanley is another excellent and experienced practitioner. If you work or live with little ones, this book might be fun to explore as she expands the philosophical repertoire beyond stories to include activities and play.

Wartenberg, Thomas, *Big Ideas for Little Kids: Teaching Philosophy through Children's Literature*. Lanham, MD: Rowman & Littlefield, 2014.
Wartenberg has developed some marvelous resources for teachers and parents to make use of traditional children's stories to promote philosophical thinking. A professional philosopher himself, his ideas are well grounded in the traditional concepts of philosophy and can serve to bridge the gap for the novice who might find it hard to locate the philosophical themes and questions in children's stories. In many ways, his work inspired this book.

Worley, Peter, *The If Machine*. New York: Continuum, 2011.
Worley, based in England, has produced a delightful and inspirational series of books on doing philosophy with children and young people. This is one of his first and a great place to start but he and his team have put many resources online and offer workshops.

The following two articles address the connections between philosophy and fairy tales.

Stanley, Sara, "A Skills Based Approach to P4C—Philosophy, Fairy Tales, and the Foundational Stage." *Gifted Educational*, Vol. 22, 2007, pp. 172–181.

Stanley offers a four-week model of using fairy tales to encourage young children to learn to think big, be flexible and open to new ideas, ask questions, and connect characters with issues and ideas that matter to the children.

Tesar, Marek, David W. Kuperman, Sophia Rodriquez, and Sonja Arndt, "'Forever Young' Childhoods, Fairy Tales and Philosophy." *Global Studies of Childhood*, Vol. 6 (2), 2016, pp. 222–233.

This team examines how fairy tales and modern stories inspired by the genre shape and mold children based on implicit models of childhood. This article is more theoretical and cautionary in tone as the authors remind us that there are subtexts under any story that can assume, presume, and color how the audience receives it. What coded messages are conveyed in these children stories and how ought we to be aware of them so as to recognize the models therein?

Appendix B

Contemporary Reimaginings of Classic Fairy Tales

There are many "fractured fairy tales" available. These are versions that have a twist in characters, setting, and often the ending. The following is a selection of some delightful picture books aimed at young children that offer familiar fairy tales with a twist.

Dodd, Emma, *Cinderelephant*. London, UK: Templar Publishing, 2012.
Emmett, Jonathan, *The Princess and the Pig*. London: Bloomsbery, 2011.
Geist, Ken, *Three Little Fish and the Big Bad Shark*. New York: Cartwheel Books, 2007.
Hale, Bruce, *Snoring Beauty*. Boston: HMH Books for Young Readers, 2008.
Jackson, Ellen, *Cinder Edna*. New York: HarperCollins, 1998.
Munsch, Robert, *The Paperbag Princess*. Toronto: Annick Press, 1981.
Schwartz, Corey Rosen, *Ninja Red Riding Hood*. New York: G. P. Putnam's Sons Books for Young Readers, 2014.
Scieszka, Jon, *The True Story of the Three Little Pigs*. London: Puffin Books, 1996.
Underwood, Deborah, *Interstellar Cinderella*. San Francisco: Chronicle Books, 2015.
Willems, Mo, *Goldilocks and the Three Dinosaurs*. New York: Balzer + Bray, 2012
Yim, Natasha, *Goldy Luck and the Three Pandas*. Watertown, MA: Charlesbridge, 2015

A recent book worth mentioning is the retelling of the *Cinderella* story by Rebecca Solnit in which she uses the classic illustrations by Arthur Rackham but for her very contemporary version where Cinderella ends up rescuing the prince and they decide to be friends and equals.

Solnit, Rebecca, *Cinderella Liberator*. Chicago: Haymarket Books, 2019.

Appendix C

Themes in Each Fairy Tale

Beauty and the Beast

Beauty
Being a Beast
Outcast/Being Left Out
Outer/Inner Beauty
Promises
Siblings and Jealousy

Cinderella

Birds
Choosing Friends/Partners
Jealousy
Loyalty
Patterns of Three
Sacrifice
Sisters

Fitcher's Bird

Curiosity
Danger
Evil
Fear
Strangers

The Frog King or Iron Heinrich

Beauty
Changing One's Mind
Exchanges
Faithfulness
Frogs
Making Promises
Rewards

Hansel and Gretel

Being Lost
Being Resourceful
Brothers and Sisters
Forests
Loyalty
Playing Tricks
Poverty
Stealing
Witches

The Little Mermaid

Adventure
Being Different
The Power of Having a Voice
Rejection
Wishing

Little Red Riding Hood

Kindness
Learning a Lesson
Strangers
Trust
Wolves

Master Cat or Puss 'n Boots

Cats
Deception
Friends
Intentions/Consequences

Lying
Materialism
Success and What Matters

Rapunzel

Compromise
Obedience
Parental Responsibility
The Power of Hair
Theft
Towers and the Double Standard

The Seven Ravens

Journey
Misbehaving
Ravens and Birds
Responsibility
Sacrifice
Wishes

Snow White

Beauty and Its Price
Cannibalism
Waiting for the Prince?
Women's/Men's Roles

The Story of the Three Bears

Animals and People
Curiosity and Manners
Getting Things Just Right
Numbers and the Theme of Three

The White Snake

Animals and People
Blame
Challenges, Trials, and Fairness
Kindness
Language
Wisdom and Knowledge

Some Notes on Our Sources

The Annotated Brothers Grimm edited by Maria Tartar; New York: W.W. Norton & Company, 2004, 2012.
This book has marvelous illustrations and lots of marginalia notes to offer background on the story as well as sharing interpretations by psychologists and folktale scholars. This includes forty-three tales from the Grimm brothers as well as nine more that are described as "for adults," perhaps due to their violence and tragic nature. The fairy tale scholar Maria Tartar has written an excellent essay on the history of the tales and the novelist A. S. Byatt wrote the introduction.

Beauty and the Beast—Classic Tales about Animal Brides and Grooms from around the World edited by Maria Tatar; New York: Penguin Books, 2017.
This book is divided into four sections: model couples from ancient times, charismatic couples in the popular imagination, animal grooms, and animal brides. Each section collects a wide array of ancient myths, classic fairy tales of many different cultures from around the world. The unifying theme is the animal/human connection.

Hans Christian Andersen—The Complete Fairy Tales and Stories, translated by Erik Christian Haugaard; New York: Anchor Books, 1983 edition.
This is a huge text but offers a great selection of fairy tales from Andersen. One of the unique aspects about him is he consciously crafted his fairy tales, rather than inheriting them from earlier sources.

The Classic Fairy Tales, edited by Maria Tatar; New York: Norton Critical Edition 1999.

This text presents eight fairy tales as they appear in a wide range of cultures, including some contemporary retellings. It also includes a hefty selection of essays and commentaries by well-known scholars, which can stimulate some critical thinking for adults and teens about the nature of fairy tales.

The Complete First Edition of the Original Folk and Fairy Tales of the Brothers Grimm, translated and edited by Jack Zipes; Princeton, NJ: Princeton University Press, 2014.

This book is relatively recent and includes all the tales from the very first edition of the Brothers Grimm collections. Included are notes and an excellent opening essay by scholar Jack Zipes about the history of the brothers and the over eight editions they published in the nineteenth century.

The Great Fairy Tale Tradition, selected and edited by Jack Zipes. New York: Norton Critical Edition, 2001.

Zipes is one of the foremost scholars of fairy tales and this collection sorts tales by themes. Tales by Straparola, Basile, and the Grimm brothers dominate, but you can find some less-known authors as well in this volume. It includes an excellent collection of critical essays as the last section.

About the Author

Wendy C. Turgeon teaches philosophy to undergraduates at St. Joseph's College, New York, and for years taught a course at Stony Brook University to graduate students in philosophy with children. She has published in the field of philosophy for/with children and presented at conferences for many years. Her other areas of interest are aesthetics, environmental ethics, and medieval philosophy.

Alice V. Gerhardstein (illustrator) earned a degree in English from Mary Washington University and an MFA in poetry from Naropa University in Bolder, Colorado. A certified organic gardener she has farmed all over the United States, worked with developmentally challenged young adults and adults, and currently lives in North Carolina.

www.ingramcontent.com/pod-product-compliance
Lightning Source LLC
Chambersburg PA
CBHW070641300426
44111CB00013B/2208